Delusion

Aliens, Cults, Propaganda and
the Manipulation of the Mind

First published by O Books, 2009
O Books is an imprint of John Hunt Publishing Ltd., The Bothy, Deershot Lodge, Park Lane, Ropley,
Hants, SO24 0BE, UK
office1@o-books.net
www.o-books.net

Distribution in:

UK and Europe
Orca Book Services
orders@orcabookservices.co.uk
Tel: 01202 665432 Fax: 01202 666219
Int. code (44)

USA and Canada
NBN
custserv@nbnbooks.com
Tel: 1 800 462 6420 Fax: 1 800 338 4550

Australia and New Zealand
Brumby Books
sales@brumbybooks.com.au
Tel: 61 3 9761 5535 Fax: 61 3 9761 7095

Far East (offices in Singapore, Thailand,
Hong Kong, Taiwan)
Pansing Distribution Pte Ltd
kemal@pansing.com
Tel: 65 6319 9939 Fax: 65 6462 5761

South Africa
Alternative Books
altbook@peterhyde.co.za
Tel: 021 555 4027 Fax: 021 447 1430

Text copyright Philip Gardiner 2008

Design: Stuart Davies

ISBN: 978 1 84694 250 1

A CIP catalogue record for this book is available
from the British Library.

Printed by Digital Book Print

O Books operates a distinctive and ethical publishing philosophy in
all areas of its business, from its global network of authors to
production and worldwide distribution.

Delusion

Aliens, Cults, Propaganda and
the Manipulation of the Mind

Philip Gardiner

BOOKS

Winchester, UK
Washington, USA

CONTENTS

Introduction

Colin Wilson

When the writer Henry Miller returned home to New York in 1940, he set out to summarise his impressions of America in a book called *The Air-Conditioned Nightmare*. Its title tells us all we need to know about his feelings about America after a decade spent in Europe. He hated it.

More than half a century later, Miller's title is a good summary of the views of Philip Gardiner, the author of the present book, on our civilisation. But we need to add an important qualification, which is to be found in the following paragraph of his first chapter:

> 'Fear is now so complex that it is a paradox in our so-called ordered society. But we need to strip away all the myriad excuses we come up with to replace the word fear and realize that it all revolves around the loss of self. It is in fact the sickness at the heart of consciousness and overcoming this one core principle will set you truly free onto a road without delusions. The reason? Because we create delusions to escape it and the marketing men of the world use every chance they can get to pull finely woven threads from our fears and form webs that trap us. If you overcome fear, then you will realize that your life has been spent in a web, created from your own emotions.'

As we can see, Gardiner is far less pessimistic than Henry Miller. That is largely because he is a better thinker – in fact, Miller is hardly a thinker at all. Gardiner sets out to analyse how we got ourselves into this mess, and he begins by asking how we came to create civilisation. Our ancestors were nomads who followed

1

their food – the herds – across the great plains. Periodically they came to a halt, and had to take the first simple steps in creating comfort. And it was then the complications began...

The complications eventually led to the emergence of one of the major villains of this book, the 'marketing man', whose schemes and inventions make us increasingly passive, and therefore create an odd feeling of frustration that we cannot detach ourselves enough to understand. For if our civilisation produces an endless stream of products designed to keep us satisfied, then how can we be unhappy?

It so happens that Gardiner was himself at one time a highly successful marketing man, and therefore knew about their techniques from the inside. It was this that made him decide to retire from it and start thinking about the mess. It made him realise that some of the marketing ploys can be as dangerous as elephant traps. His chapter (6) on the Internet contains examples of some attempted swindles that would be funny if they were not so insidious – letters offering us vast sums of money if we will go into a partnership that involves merely acting as agents and taking charge of funds that will then flood into our bank accounts... (I myself usually receive a least one a week.)

All this sheer mass of complexity tends to overwhelm us and erode our sense of freedom. And what is freedom? The inventor Buckminster Fuller put his finger on it when he remarked 'I seem to be a verb'. And when we feel 'like verbs', seething with vital energy, we instinctively understand who we are and what life is about.

In the last decade of his life, the French novelist Flaubert decideed to write a novel that would summarise everything he disliked about modern life. It would be about two copying clerks called Bouvard and Pecuchet, who fall into conversation as they sit on a bench and realise how much they have in common. Both feel that life has cheated them by tying them to a desk, and both long to expand their knowledge of the world. Now they will move in together, and set out to learn everything their education has denied them, all about art and science and history. When one of them is left a fortune, they spend their days sitting facing one another at a desk and passing on to each other remarkable pieces of information about the real world. 'Only phenomena are true' they declare. And of course, the result is sheer chaos, an avalanche of meaningless facts.

How can we fight our way out of this avalanche? What is necessary is a certain knowledge about the force of evolution. The author'sexcelent summary goes:

'Professor James Gardner, a peer reviewed philosopher of universal law said in *What is Enlightenment* magazine that the universe is intelligent at the subatomic level and that it acts like a DNA feedback loop. DNA, as it instructs cells to grow is fed back information by the cell at the quantum level and it then uses this information and sends back further instructions. It is believed that the universe does this also and that we are part of the cellular structure feeding information back into the universal DNA and then receiving new instructions. We are all connected to everything via quantum particle entanglement – we just don't know it. We are in fact conscious beings at a level of existence that is mathematically in perfect balance with the universe and we are at the very center of this structure. There are as many atoms within us as there are stars in the universe – we are perfectly centered in the greater cosmic soup. In fact it would take as many humans to make the mass of our very own sun, as there are atoms within us – and so we are at the very center of our solar system. We are connected perfectly to the universe both at the quantum level and the mathematical harmonious level – it is perfection created from chaos.'

This is the answer to the chaos that entraps Bouvard and

Pecuchet, and that left Henry Miller feeling that we are living in an air-conditoned nightmare. Miller felt that way because he was no thinker. But Philip Gardiner *is* a thinker, and is not intimidated by the problem. And in this stimulating, vigorously written book, he demonstrates that no one needs to be intimidated – provided he is willing to use his mind for the purpose it was intended.

Preface

Fear

This book is the result of an awakening. It is the same awakening to the self and to the wonder of the cosmos that has driven thinking men and women for generations. It is the same awakening that has been the generative cause of the affect of religion and belief. It is the same awakening that has then caused man to revolt against the same. It is the awakening that has been written, painted, sculptured, symbolized and placed into music for thousands of years. From mythology to etymology, this opening up of the mind to the potentials of the human spirit has been known about ever since man began to think. And yet, now in the 21st century mankind has created more chains to bind himself than at any point in human history.

From the very beginning mankind has sought to free his mind from the constraints of a consciousness that seemed to bind him into a world divided. The animals around him followed natural cycles and marched thousands of miles in-tune with the breath of the earth, the phases of the moon and the warmth of the sun. Man pondered these remarkable phenomena, because he was now aware of it and this awareness gave him the need to explain it. Without explanation everything seemed strange and he therefore feared it. What man did not understand, he could not control and lack of control and understanding meant simply one thing – chaos. The consciousness of the mind needed order to survive and so he began to form structures within his thoughts for all things. He gave symbols and words to everything that previously didn't need them. The bird didn't care that it was a bird; the fish just were and the lions were boss in their own domain. The mind of man came along and gave them all names and forced them and himself into ordered boxes. This simply led to constraint and man had begun to form his own prison. He made names for leaders, gave them wonder and awe; he created gods and deities and worshipped them; he ordered his tribe and family structures and at the end of all this he had developed dogma, doctrine, rules and regulations. Man had made a world of control and he had no understanding of what he had done. Now thousands and thousands of years later our ordering of everything has created a chaotic mess – the direct opposite of what we had intended with our conscious mind. The animals, without self-awareness and higher consciousness still have their natural and ordinary lives. They do not fear not having this or that - they just exist. They, like all things natural, find balance. We, with our millennia of striving to order our lives have created chaos and now billions of people are messed up and seeking re-connection to nature.

The reason for the failure of our attempts is simple – we are out of step with nature. The route to our own true nature is to be found in the unconscious world of the mind – for in there our true self resides, hiding like a lost child. We are not aware of this because we are unconscious of it – it's that simple. Our conscious mind is almost an unnatural thing, in that it fights with nature because of fear. We all know that we are born and that we die. We know that we exist and so we therefore have a personality – we are individual. This individual is precious to us, because we believe it is *us*. The fear comes when we realize that this individual will one day die and so it is not the fear of death itself, but the loss of the self. We have created wondrous imaginative answers to this problem however by explaining to our own minds that our body is not really us and that it is simply a container, carrying the self. When this container withers and rots, the true self or soul, shall carry on after death and be transported to heaven, nirvana or any other amazing realm perceived and fashioned by our ancestors. It is a triumph of consciousness – a prize of logical thought – that in the first place we became aware of our own frailties and then "discovered" that it was all just a minor test on the road to St Peter's pearly gates.

Today, in the 21st century as the old fashioned concepts of religion are constantly bombarded by new empowered free thinkers and science we are finding new ways of explaining our lot – for the fear of the nihilistic mind is still one that strikes a discord, even in the mind of the most erudite brains. Anything from cloning and freezing our bodies to superior alien minds and quantum oneness are being trumpeted out for our choosing. From the physical to the metaphysical, like the shopping malls of downtown LA, we can choose an answer that suits our own personal life, peer group and sense of right and wrong. The driving force, regardless of century is still the same – fear.

It seems that no matter how high we climb on the awareness ladder, the same driving force in the consciousness arises and the same forces of nature surge beneath the surface in the unconscious realm. If the animals move and are driven by the forces of nature – something hidden within our unconscious world – then we as conscious and confused beings are at odds with this drive. It is a drive hidden in the dark world of the mind – the part we can no longer access with ease – and it is something that we seemingly cannot control. Because of our disjointed life with the unconscious world of nature we fear it.

Fear is now so complex that it is a paradox in our so-called ordered society. But we need to strip away all the myriad excuses we come up with to replace the word fear and realize that it all revolves around the loss of self. It is in fact the sickness at the heart of consciousness and overcoming this one core principle will set you truly free onto a road without delusions. The reason? Because we create delusions to escape it and the marketing men of the world use every chance they can get to pull finely woven threads from our fears and form webs that trap us. If you overcome fear, then you will realize that your life has been spent in a web, created from your own emotions.

All forms of fear are ugly and create ugly offspring. We see these as separate kinds of fear, but they are all from the same parent. This must not be confused with respect, which is the healthy version. I respect the roaring lion, I do not fear it. My respect, through understanding, means that I will not place "myself" in danger by stepping in front of a hungry lion.

Fear, however, breeds and breeds. It spreads from you to your children; it evolves and transmutes. It creates prejudice and hatred. Fear is constantly used to manipulate our thoughts, our purchases, our votes and our wallets. We need only watch the television commercials to see how fear is used to control our actions. But, we only have ourselves to blame for handing over the control of our mind to this fear factor. We need to take back control – these are our thoughts and nobody else's. The only way to freedom is through *personal integrity* and *honesty* – not with anybody else, but with ourselves. If we are not truly honest with ourselves then we are simply creating yet more illusions to overcome. If we know that we are deluding ourselves by going to Church on Sunday, or buying happiness during "retail" therapy, then we add guilt and confusion on top of fear. We all do this most of the time and this is why life inside the mind has become so complicated and why we have come so far away from nature itself.

Half of the problem is the evolutionary childhood drive to learn. Misunderstanding this process – or not even realizing it is there – has caused immense trouble. You see as we grow we have an in-built drive to learn and this can cause a slight inferiority complex – i.e. that we do not know as much as our parents and so we feel inferior. This can stifle the self and causes us to take on personality as well as knowledge. As long as the knowledge is useful, valid and valuable then it is fine. But if the knowledge is worthless and even poisonous then we are in effect poisoning our minds. Adding the personality of the parent or teacher or other influence is yet again distancing us from who we are and our connections to nature. This drive continues with us even past childhood and is yet another evolutionary drive utilized by the marketing man. A simple example is to take a screen hero – let's say James Bond. We go to the cinema and watch this brave, handsome and intellectual man save the world. We admire these things and so we try to emulate them – to take on a Bond persona. In the 1950's many females did the same with Doris Day films. In fact none of these characters were real. Doris Day was acting and Bond is the creation of an alter ego by the writer Ian Fleming, who drank and smoked himself to death at an early age. The point is, that we attempt to copy or mirror an ideal that is itself flawed because it was created by a human mind, and so we fall short, as we all must. This leads to yet further elements of inferiority and lack of self worth. A great many neuroses and psychological problems are caused by lack of understanding of this evolutionary drive and the parent's inability to see this and teach or train accordingly.

This book is about the awakening of the self to the world of delusion that we have created, that we live in and that we force one another still deeper into each and every day. Never in the history of man has there been a perfect time and so we need not seek out a sunken Atlantis. Never in the future of mankind will there be a perfect civilization and so we better not sit and wait for Star Trek to fix things for us. No one religion is righteous all fall short of the glory they call God. No State has created the ideal place to live. No family is flawless, no friend wholly committed. We are the best thing we have. We have to live with ourselves, others can run away from us or lock us in a room. We will be in that room with our self and so that is where we must find the truth and that is where we must discover balance and harmony. Listening to the world of man will simply confuse our minds yet further. Listening to nature, which has perfect balance and indeed is powered by the force of balance, is the right place to go for help. We must return to the garden.

Chapter 1

Present Madness

This is an economic world. It is structured around money and anything that gets in the way of the machine is more often than not moved or eradicated. There is no room for anything to oppose this. Each one of us is in the system whether we like it or not and we believe there is often precious little we can do about it. But how did all this begin? And who was the originator of the system?

In the beginning mankind was nomadic. For a period so long that it staggers the mind we traveled along coastlines, around lakes and traversed river systems. We simply could not travel across land because most of it was covered in trees and vegetation. We did so purely to hunt and collect foodstuffs and then returned to our boats. This is the way and form mankind evolved his mind over vast periods of time. But how was man able to navigate over the sea? This is an open question and is the subject of much debate. He certainly watched the stars, sun and moon. He placed markers along the way, but he also had an in-built homing mechanism – a sense of direction – now mostly lost to us due to the confusion of the modern society and modern mind. There are many scientific test results, which confirm that man does have the ability, probably via his pineal organ, to judge direction intuitively. This ability is due to the electromagnetic energy of the earth and the magnetic connection between it and the pineal organ within the brain in exactly the same way that a bird uses magnetite within its pineal organ to pick up the electro-magnetic resonance. In short, mankind had connection to the world around him and this is just one way in which we were more in-tune with our environment. But we were in-tune in other ways too – we were in-tune with our needs and natures larder.

We followed herds as they migrated; we knew which plants were safe to eat and we only took what we needed because we simply could not carry an overabundance of produce. All the anthropological evidence reveals that mankind was more peaceful and even lived longer lives than his later descendents who would settle down.

There is evidence from author Crichton E. M. Miller, that mankind developed tools for navigation too. Miller found that for thousands of years mankind watched the stars and developed specific tools in the form of circles and crosses to map the planets, stars and constellations and this became a holy writ. Evidence of this is found in stone circles, carvings in ancient caves and religious icons such as the Celtic Cross. Anybody who wishes to understand this ancient knowledge at a deeper level should read Miller's extraordinary book, *The Golden Thread of Time*. But the point is, that man needed to navigate, because it was his way of life for eons and today's static and settled situation is in stark contrast to this natural in-tune order.

Eventually it appears that populations grew and nomadic cultures began to partly settle down. These settlements were probably originally staging posts for extended stays during winter or other such times and eventually the rot set it. Remaining in one location for extended periods brought with it allmanner of problems. Firstly it brought the need to cultivate the land and to store provisions because the animal larder would carry on moving and natural vegetation would carry on and follow the seasons. Secondly it brought disease because of human and animal waste and all kinds of other filth. And thirdly it brought strife in ways that the nomadic smaller groups would not have foreseen. These settlements would be attracting more and more people into one single location – forcing people together for longer and longer periods of time, in cramped and rapidly unnatural environments. Mankind was growing apart from nature and had to learn a whole set of new skills, from building to being more socially oriented. Structures of wood and structures of society brought with them hierarchy and alpha dominance in a different way to the previous nomadic lifestyle. Groups were now bigger and so conflicts between those who would be in dominance would have been more frequent. But it was too late, the old ways were rapidly being forgotten. It is amazing how quickly the skills of the past generation can disappear. For example, today there are people who do not even know how to cook because their lifestyle has simply never called for the skill. We are constantly battling the balance between the income stream and the spending stream and we find very little room for such trivial matters as cooking, let alone time for our children. But cooking is only one of the many skills that we are losing due to mass production of ready-made meals and lifestyle habits. In England, and I am sure this is true of many nations, even schools had to be legislated to bring back real cooked food.

Eventually though our new found settlements had to find ways to deal with their new social problems and the mind of man has a unique tool for the purpose – imagination. Man developed, from within his own imagination, new social structures of tribal leadership and those who had maintained or learned new skills important for the group would become dominant. These were not always the strongest and best fighters or hunters, but more often than not those who knew how to heal and gel the community. We call these people medicine men, shaman and latterly priests. As the Old Testament so eruditely informs us, it was the priesthood who would guide the people and even crown kings. The Royal family of England is still to this day crowned by the Church as a direct result of this same ancient power structure – uniting religion and State.

With this new advent of power came many new ways of manipulating the growing masses who were herded into the new imaginative religious structure and given rules in the form of dogma, doctrine and tradition. Now power was from the gods and nobody could argue with such imagined power. The knowledge of navigation, of the stars, of the seasons and of course of the reality of the mind of man became powerful tools in the armory of the Church. To know the seasons enabled the priest to appear magical and in-touch with god. To know how to read the stars for navigation enabled the tribe to trade and invade. To know the mind of man allowed the priesthood to manipulate and control. All of this was truly a powerful knowledge. This knowledge was passed down within the brotherhoods in symbolism, latterly in texts and certainly in tradition.

Tradition is not simply something we imagine our grandparents had. It is not just something those stuffy looking pompous Englishmen re-enact everyday in Parliament or that wonderfully colorful changing of the guard outside the gates of Buckingham Palace.

Our English term tradition comes from *Traditio*, a Latin word meaning the 'delivery of doctrine' and 'surrender', but more pertinent to us it means 'something handed down.' There is depth here as many will know, for this 'something handed down' is not just the old pocket watch that our ancestors sported in the 19th century and has been passed from one generation to another. No, tradition is also the continuance of something much more profound, much more in-tune with the *Da Vinci Code* concept of the bloodline.

In the very first usage of the word we find that it was in fact used *for the passing on of doctrine and religious dogma* - a sacred act itself and something which became symbolic. The word 'sacred' itself comes from Old Latin *saceres* meaning to bind, restrict, enclose and protect. And this is where much of the truth lies - in symbolism and sacredness, for both are binding and surrendering to something being passed down. The acts of those parliamentarians and the guard at Buckingham Palace are symbolic and sacred acts, representing something other than the physical and literal things we see. The same is true of religious tradition.

There is no truth that the taking of the bread and wine at the Eucharist ritual - a tradition seen across the world - actually is the body and blood of Jesus Christ. No, the act is symbolic and solemnly reminds the religious initiate of the fact that he is part of a greater Christian brotherhood; that he is accepting Christ and that His body was broken and blood spilt for us and that he is a *continuation of a long line*. Whatever ones opinion on that religious act, the fact remains that it is a very powerful tool for reminding the masses of their place in the world via an act that is emotionally strong. This is a manipulating tradition, kept alive to keep the sheep in the fold.

As we can now see, tradition can be a very strong device when allied to emotion and psychologists have discovered that allegorical tales are very often absorbed better than any literal telling.

In this allegorical or symbolic respect there are other words that also relate and of which we should take note. These words now often hold mystery to us, because we have lost the meaning of them, as we have all too often lost the meaning of tradition. Myth, fable, tale, story - all these, and more, are used in the 'traditional' way to pass on hidden or esoteric knowledge from one generation to another. And this is a 'tradition' going back in time for thousands of years - the custom of the storyteller, whose job it was to keep alive the truths of the tribe. From the medicine man and shaman to druid, Brahman and later Catholic priest, we have entrusted our social history and religious emotional beliefs to the wise-man of the tribe or culture. Held within the many myths, fables, tales and stories are a great many truths awaiting the key to unlock them again. And many of these truths are symbolic codes, hiding a secret belief that the contemporary religious authority would have looked down upon.

And I am of the opinion that with a new set of eyes we can ourselves find the keys to unlock these historical conundrums – as Crichton Miller uncovered the navigational truths of the cross and circle. We have to understand our ancestors were able to do this and we have to start by realizing that they were humans just like us. They had fears, hopes and struggled to survive and to comprehend their very place in the universe. In the depth of understanding our ancestors discovered that they needed to find a way of passing on the knowledge they had uncovered and they formed tales. Our historical friends were not simple folk as we are led to believe. They had the same brain size as ourselves and in fact in many ways they were better attuned to the thing we now divisively call *nature*. You see, in our 'modern' materialistic state we forget that we are human beings that have come from and live in the natural universe. We forget, because we create things from within our own imaginations and surround ourselves with them, and hence we today find ourselves in an imaginary world of 'things.' This *PC* in front of me is formed from the imagination of thousands of individuals. In one respect it is not a natural item, but in another because it was formed from the mind of man then it is the result of that natural human factor - imagination. It is this ability of the mind to *create a concept* that has spawned stories and tales, myths and fables to explain to each new generation the knowledge of the last. And so what is the key we need to understand these concepts? It is imagination in tune with intuition *or our connection to nature.*

Tradition is a treasure chest of esoteric secrets awaiting the imagination of some bright spark to find the key and unlock it. If 'tradition' is that thing handed down from one generation to another, then it is our duty to find the key. And today that key lies in the quantum world. For within the all-too peculiar world of quantum physics what we shall discover is the connection through time of our own bloodline, our own thoughts and patterns, passing on through time and connected to the great matrix of the mind of the universe. As we share huge percentages of our DNA with our fellow animals and plants, so too we share a universal quantum connection - we are indeed entangled at the sub-atomic particle level to all reality - not just now, but for all time - and this quantum reality may very well be intelligent.

Tradition may have hidden this peculiar knowledge in symbolism and sacred texts and called it God. It is time to understand *tradition* afresh and to understand the *sacred* nature of humanity and consciousness. For in so doing we shall see all-manner of things hidden there by our ancestors and be better able to understand ourselves. It is not a bad thing to realize that we are in fact directly linked via genetics and maybe even quantum physics to the mind of the first man and woman.

These incredible and intuitive 'traditions' then, emerged from early man and his understanding of the world around him and how he survived. But all was not well in mankind's early settled Eden's and differences of opinion would often arise between settled groups or tribes and not least of these differences was jealousy. This distinctly negative element of the human mind would involve jealousy over land, produce, mates and of course the still relevant modern problem of jealousy over holy sites. However, trade also played a big part in the greater mix and so tribes grew steadily more and more wealthy in terms of possessions as each area had its own special supply of salt, gold, animals, plants and even access routes to the more distant lands. This was the birth of our modern system many thousands of years ago – built upon an unnatural desire to remain in one location and yet also built upon the natural desire to be the best – one of the strongest evolutionary drives.

Settlements became trading posts for vast quantities of goods and demarcation of roles emerged with blacksmiths, farmers, potters and all-manner of other roles. Trading went on like this for millennia, with the priesthood often controlling the process and growing in power themselves as their own communities prospered. They would take a percentage of the produce and offer it to the gods in-order to maintain the weather and good fortune of the tribe. The greatest of gods – the sun – would be worshipped and aided in its journey to reappear the following day. It was the giver of life and the destroyer. It mirrored the duality in the mind of man himself and so we were formed in his likeness. We were solar beings, formed and given life by the power of the golden orb and nothing became more important than ensuring its daily and yearly cycles. The priests of this great power were the alpha males, the medicine men or shaman of earlier times. It was they who gave authority to the king or pharaoh who himself must be the son of the sun on earth. He was the marketing tool of the priesthood and history is awash with the violent downfalls of the solar king when he stepped out of line and upset the priesthood.

Markets emerged near or even in Temples and bustled with people and produce of the wider world. Social commerce also emerged as priesthood's shared or traded knowledge with other cultures and soon belief systems across vast continents had little to set them apart. Much of this knowledge or tradition was very important and of value to the community and involved knowledge of astrology and astronomy to enable them to predict the seasons and for navigation. As the power base of trade grew, so the ability to navigate became extremely important and as the majority of the population had forgotten how to do this, it emerged as a special knowledge guarded closely by the elite.

Control of the trading markets, both of the land upon which it was carried out and the navigation required to operate it, grew so powerful over time that the priesthood would do almost anything to maintain control. This is why much religious literature is awash with rules and regulations for trade and commerce. The system of trading eventually needed organizing differently because of lies. It all began because of deceit and it remains pretty much the same today. At the market a thing called a promise emerged whereby a man trading a goat for a pig would promise to bring his goat the following market day only to fail in his promise. The priesthood or leader who controlled the process realized that some new system was needed to come into play and so created money – from the word *monere*, meaning "to warn."

This new money was very cleverly based upon the gods themselves adding incredible weight and fear to the promise. Gold was manifestly the solar divinity – the sun. And silver was the lunar deity – a mirror of the sun. Handing over a symbolic representation of the gods was a powerful promise and the gods would know if you reneged on your promise. The Church itself backed the promise and so became the bank. Power was well and truly in the hands of the few and the rest of us simply had no choice but to conform. This situation is almost unchanged and today many banks are at least still partly owned by various Churches – not least of which is the Catholic Church.

Our lives are still and more so than ever run by money and we have no choice but to live in the world of commerce. Everyday we hand over our images of the solar deities, which are no longer even real gold but instead are promises of gold. There are more promises of gold in the world than there is gold and so the system, created because of lies and deceit, is itself a total lie. But it is the system we live in and individually we must make our own decisions on how to do so. But there is more deception than we know and it is to these deceptions we must now turn.

Chapter 2

Deception

From the moment we wake up to the moment we fall asleep we are subjects of a massive machine. We are plugged in like a light that is only alive and lit by the machine and because of this we no longer know how to shine for ourselves. But many do not realize that the machine in fact feeds from us – using our energy to capture and grow the machine that in turn captures more and more people hourly. We are all in one way or another slaves to the machine.

We have seen how money enslaved us because of the lie and deceit of man and how power was built and maintained by the few over the many. Today it is the driving force of society. Every single one of us must sell something to get money. Whether we sell our skills, services, products or even our very soul, we all must constantly sell to earn. And because everybody is selling to everybody else we also buy and buy. In our overpopulated world, full of people who no longer know the skills of basic survival we must buy the basic products such as food and even water. But man has used his unique imagination to make better and more imaginative food and water – or so we believe. In fact we dress up the ordinary and use our own in-built psychology to convince others that this added value is worth the extra money. We place a clever label on a bottle of water, add mystique and then charge a ridiculous amount of money for what is basically a free product of the earth that we can no longer have access to as individuals because of the society we have created. We do the same for all-manner of goods.

In addition to this we also create products or services that we do not need and again add value or perception that we want to buy into.

In order to understand how we are lead down this path we must see into the mind of the marketing man. As I am in the unique position of having been one of the successful marketing men, then this understanding is coming to you directly from the source.

Many marketing men will tell you that they need to understand the product or service in-depth. This is true only in the sense that the marketing man needs to know to whom the product has to be sold. He defines the primary market sector and then secondary sectors and very often will have multiple level campaigns. Let's take an example. Let's assume we need to sell a product to children. There are a great many ways to the market, but our purpose here is to see how we as humans are manipulated into action or sometimes inaction. To sell to children sometimes we may need to go through the desires and perceptions of the parents, however let's assume we are targeting the children themselves. Firstly we have to assume a product and for this simple illustration let's assume a new candy bar. In the first place we have to make sure the packaging is right. Our inner desire to eat candy is in fact perfectly natural and is based upon the need for fruit, which of course feeds the body's need for vitamins and glucose. Unfortunately the candy bar overfeeds us sugar and not glucose or vitamins and so defeats the object and in fact simply leaves us craving more because the body firstly, is not getting what it needs and secondly, there are often chemicals within the bar that are short and long term addictive.

So with this knowledge of the marketing man simply dresses the candy bar up to look like fruit or whatever natural product or part of our diet it is replacing. In addition to this there is the hormone process, which must be taken into account. The different ages of man produce different levels of hormones. When we are younger our natural drives and desires are stronger and more acute. This means that when we are younger we are more primary and so primary colors, shapes, sounds and smells are used. This is of course a generalization and not every individual is the same and this is indicative of how we are all placed into boxes throughout our lives – creating more unnatural states of existence and distancing us yet further from our own intuition. The marketing man's statistical data does in fact reveal that these uses of primary devices on children and young adults consistently delivers good results. The reverse of this is often true of the elderly generations, who prefer more pastel colors and softer shapes and sounds.

We can see then in this simple demonstration how we can again fall into the traps of lies and deceit by our own hormones, desires and drives and the manipulation of the machine. This manipulation has been in existence for thousands of years and mankind, from the priesthood to the State, has learned how to use this to control us. The common folk of Europe, who were kept humble and illiterate for generations, were fed mass propaganda in stained glass windows and with the pageantry of State occasions. All of this, and more, fed the story chosen by the elite few, to the masses and the masses absolved themselves of responsibility by following.

The next element our marketing man must include is a thing known as a branding device. This is not necessarily a corporate identity as corporations have many products and each one must have its own branding identity. If we take our fictional candy bar it may very well carry the corporate logo, which is a symbol of the corporation. This can add value to the product if the corporation has a strong identity and can pull upon the emotions of the individual purchasing the product with the tribal sense of loyalty – brand or corporate loyalty. This is the exact same as loyalty to the Church or State and again absolves the individual of responsibility for what he is eating or indeed feeding to his children. This absolution is false, as we all hold responsibility for our own actions. Just because x corporation is big and has been around for a long time does not mean that it is perfect. Far from it, the corporation is still run by humans out for greed and growth. We tend to forget that several big brand companies in fact started by selling us drugs or making weapons.

The emotions and ties to the corporation must firstly therefore be ones of trust in the corporation and its products. Any corporation that loses this trust factor is on a slippery slope and will have to go through a period of self recreation in the market place to re-establish itself or even re-brand itself. One thing corporations, States and religions fear the most is the powerful word of mouth, which spreads bad news on the "Devil's Radio" of gossip like wild-fire. This is the power of the individual against the control of the few and is one reason that corporations attempt to appear under a disguise and therefore independent on the internet.

Once we have a strong corporate identity we must then brand the candy bar dependent upon the selected market place. Some candy bars are in fact retro-branded to attract both children and the sense of history and tradition embedded in the older generations – allowing the person to recapture their youth, a time always emotionally tied and often imaginary.

The branding of a product will go through a series of market tests with a specially selected group and the results collated. This may happen several times but in each case the marketing man will be looking for emotional results. This all pulls upon our deepest desires and nothing is stronger than the utilization of emotions. Religion, politics and corporate greed has used emotional responses for a very long time. In the end, marketing is about the psychology of man and whoever best understands the mind of man will succeed in the financial stakes.

Once the product has been branded and packaged according to all these criteria and more, the next step in the game is to convince the general public and the specific market sector to purchase the product and in-order to do this we have developed a very simple structure that utilizes our own psychology.

AIDA

Whether the launch of a product or a service is to be via advertising, press release or some other means the actual method is the same and again is based upon perfectly natural desires. The process is called AIDA.

A – The A stands for Attention and this is simply the method of attracting our attention in anyway possible. In a press release we may only have a few seconds of the editors time to attract his or her attention. This is an art and the press release author must have their finger on the pulse of human activity. For instance let's assume that we branded our new candy bar the Da Vinci Choco. The best time to release this would have been at the height of the *Da Vinci Code* phenomena. It would have firstly made an interesting tale for any news editor, but secondly it would have pulled upon the tribal desires of humans to be part of the wave in the same way exactly that a bird changes direction when the flock moves.

This is an in-built evolutionary protection device now being bastardized by the marketing man. It is enticing us into a dream reality based upon nature and manipulated for the desire to be the alpha dominant species. We turn this knowledge against ourselves and end up as extensions of a statistic, dehumanized, sterile and eventually unhappy because our desires are in reality not fulfilled. Follow a dream and you end up in a dream.

Grabbing the attention of the individual, regardless of genre, is the first and most important part of marketing. Breaking down the psychology of the prospective clients and the age, sex and cultural background are important to understanding how best to attract attention. For instance with children we use vibrant colors, primary shapes, fresh and enticing smells and modern catchy music and sound bites. With the eldest generations we use pastel shades of colors, smoother shapes and retro smells and sounds. The reason for this is simple - hormones. The hormones of the individual change as time passes from strong to weak and these affect our likes and dislikes. From teen to middle ages there is a stronger sexual drive and this also comes from hormones.

Overall there are two most popular colors - red and blue. The vibrancy of these colors will alter according to the age. However, color also must be used in accordance with the product and lend an edge of meaning. For instance Macdonald's, Pepsi, Coca Cola aim at younger people - because older ones mostly know better, and so they use vibrant blues and reds. Whereas coffee shops use less vibrant and more subtle colors and themes. Both pump their "smells" out into the world!

Attention is more than just a TV advert or a brochure though. It is also about tele-sales. On the phone we have anywhere between 2 - 5 seconds to grab attention and so we have to use the same techniques but verbally. Older generations are more canny and less likely to give you time; younger ones are a little more gullible and may give you a little longer - although in all cases education and cultural backgrounds come into play. One of the best ways of grabbing and keeping attention is to ask questions – because everybody likes to talk about themselves. Pulling on these natural in-built neuroses has always been a standard controlling tool, like listening to confession. It is more than just our liking to reveal our own lives, it is also a confessional and the confessed is handing over a large part of their lives and connecting at a deeper level to the sales person. It is called "being trapped."

I – The I stands for Interest. Once we have managed to catch the editors or consumers eye with Attention we now have to keep their interest. This involves telling them something about the thing that caught their attention in an interesting way. This, more often than not, must include drama and theatrics. We have to write the press release in the correct dramatically oriented fashion for the given market place. It is a little like our attention being caught by a sudden movement in the woods. We stop for a moment and look. If we don't see another movement then we simply move on. But if we do see another movement and then another, then our eye remains and we want to know more. Again, it is all pulling upon the natural senses and instincts and *Interest* is simply more little *Attentions*.

D – D is for Desire. Once we have attracted attention and maintained interest in the prospective client, neophyte or purchaser, we have them hooked and we keep them hooked by building their desire to buy. This step means that we have to create such a desire to buy the product or service that we have them in a virtual stranglehold. They must overcome their own cravings and urges to deny this stage and that is difficult and almost impossible for a great many people to do – especially those who have no idea that they have been sold to in the first place. All of this is again based upon the strongest of human emotions. More often than not for teenagers and upwards this will include some form of sexual connotation – it being the strongest driving force (over love). It may also be tribal – creating the desire to have what the rich and famous have or indeed to be better than others and thereby stamp our perceived alpha dominance as the fittest of the bastardized species. This 'association' will give people that talking point amongst their peers, so that they can show off how incredibly clever, rich, famous, individual or just plain sexy they are. This creates an unreal world of perceptions around themselves and gradually they forget who they really are and become an image of the marketing man's mind – the perfect fool.

A – the final A is for Action. Now that we have hooked the prey in with a dream world we simply have to give them a way of achieving that dream for themselves. This is Action – the 'how' to get into dreamland. Today, with facsimile machines, telephones, shops, the internet, mail and email, there is a whole host of methods to access dreamland and any seller who does not utilize all of these is missing out. We like to think we are stating our individuality by ordering 'online' where other fools drive to the shops, and yet it is just another method of accessing retail heaven. The real individual knows himself well enough to know better.

In the end the whole process reveals how easy it can be with this special knowledge to take from another. Create a dream and then sell it and nobody realizes that they are in fact buying into exactly that – a dream from within the mind of another. It is not reality, if indeed we can decide on what reality truly is anymore. It is not needed, it is just desired because of our bastardized social norm and position. We pay more for water in a fancy bottle than the worth of both the bottle and the water and all because it may have a French and classy sounding name. This water is shipped thousands of miles to get to your door, when all along there is water almost everywhere on this planet. We pay a fortune for a ready prepared plastic bag full of salad produce that "meets with our modern lifestyles", whilst all along we fill our gardens with plastic lights, BBQ's and pretty flowers. In parallel with this, people starve in the Third World. What is reality? Ask a starving child and see if it the same as your own perception – if you truly need a personal benchmark.

Our reality, is not true reality. It is not reality and it is not needed, it is all self-perpetuating a massive lie and we all in our daily lives help to continue the cycle. We all make dreams and sell them to others and we then end up believing them ourselves and before anybody realizes it we are all living in a dream world that simply does not exist.

Chapter 3

Extensions

Now we have seen how our very nature, dreams and desires trap us and are used against us, for and by us. Nobody can now claim to be free of all of this, nor innocent of its abuse. But today there is yet another level of control upon us, and one in which we as human beings are rapidly becoming lost. It is a world of dreams in such an incredibly profound and stark fashion that we ought to be amazed that we have fallen into its gaping mouth.

As the battle to beat everybody else has ensued, it has bought all-manner of imaginative inventions. These are forms, manifested from within the mind of man. And here is an issue because one thing is sure – the mind of man is divided and at odds with not just itself, but everybody else and now nature too. We all constantly fight intense battles inside our mind. We argue with ourselves, as if there were two or more of us in there. We argue on an hourly and daily basis, trying to reason through mundane issues, but also more emotive concerns about life and death. We worry about loved ones and have to come to terms with the fact that we think of ourselves as gods and yet we suffer and die like 'mere' animals. Imagination has again stepped into the breach and we have fed ourselves yet more lies and the age-old extension of our own ego – god – as an answer to the dilemma that we may not in fact be the most important thing on the planet. All of this is a result of our divided minds and we are deluding ourselves with all-manner of answers, which never quite seem to fulfil us and close the divide. Until we fully accept what we really are we will go on creating new realities. This has been true of mankind for millennia and certainly true of him when he settled down into communities.

The technologies of today are in fact taking us further and

further away from reality and more into the dream state than ever before.

An example of this began in the 1960's when Joseph Weizenbaum, an American artificial intelligence expert developed a psychotherapy computer program called Eliza. The program was set up to simply return typed answers in a slightly different order and was so convincing people actually believed Eliza to be intelligent. Here is an example of the easy way we can be fooled into conversing with mere electrical energy and a few bits of metal, taken from *Computer Power and Human Reason* by Joseph Weizenbaum, published by W. Freeman, San Fransisco, 1976:

Patient: Men are all alike.
Eliza: In what way?
Patient: They're always bugging us about something or other.
Eliza: Can you think of a specific example?
Patient: Well, my boyfriend made me come here.
Eliza: Your boyfriend made you come here?
Patient: He says I'm depressed all the time.
Eliza: I am sorry to hear you are depressed.
Patient: It's true I am unhappy.
Eliza: Do you think coming here will help you not to be unhappy?
Patient: I need some help, that much seems certain.
Eliza: What would it mean to you if you got some help?
Patient: Perhaps I could learn to get along with my mother.
Eliza: Tell me about your family.
Patient: My mother takes care of me.
Eliza: Who else in your family takes care of you?
Patient: My father.
Eliza: Your father?
Patient: You are like my father in some way.
Eliza: What resemblance do you see?

Patient: You are not very aggressive but I don't want you to want me to notice that.

Eliza: What makes you think I am not very aggressive?

Patient: You don't argue with me.

Eliza: Why do you think I don't argue with you?

Patient: You are afraid of me.

Eliza: Does it please you to think I am afraid of you?

Patient: My father is afraid of everybody.

Eliza: What else comes to mind when you think of your father?

Patient: Bullies.

As we can see, at the very birth of computer technology mankind was attempting to become God and create intelligence. So far he has failed, but the predictions seem to suggest that one day soon we shall find ourselves face to face with our mechanical selves. Nevertheless in the decades since Eliza was created (and then closed down pretty rapidly) technology has surged ahead and become so convincing that humankind can escape into a virtually real world within the imagery and sound of computer technology.

Billions of children around the world are being fed unrealities by computer games. They live out their precious lives in a world that is not real, whilst mom and dad spend their every waking moment battling and selling to pay for the products of the delusional world. This causes yet more division within each mind but also within the family unit and because all of this is an illusion not one of them is truly fulfilled and so the family eventually breaks down and division in the form of divorce often occurs. The child is only being prepared for one thing – a life of exactly the same as his parents – a treadmill of buy and sell and lack of self-knowledge.

Instead of learning the simple basic skills of life and love, children today are taught how to manipulate the illusionary world of computer screens, moving imaginary characters around, killing and maiming the enemy, which is normally some politically propagandized and illusionary evil role-model. Most people do not realize the incredible amounts of money made from the multi-million dollar worlds of illusion, but they also don't realize the propaganda content is immense. In fact there are many war games (and others) strategically funded by governments and other agenda driven authorities and organizations that are specifically written to suck in the minds of the youth into particular ways of thinking. This creates masses of later controllable young adults for the financial war machine and good voters who are now loyal to the cause. We are all pawns in a game that has gone out of control, because it is a life spent in an illusionary world with nobody specifically controlling it anymore. We all make assumptions about our leaders, peers, corporations, State and religion – and yet, all along, they are making assumptions about us. Nobody is in control anymore – for nobody ever was. It is simply all the world of the dream state, created over time by one thing and another, without a goal or purpose other than bastardized functions of the evolutionary mind.

Now we have a world of technology that is overtaking us and we have to somehow try to keep our heads wrapped around the lightning speed with which it moves. There are even extensions to the computer game dream world, as with mobile phones we can in fact take this world of illusion with us anywhere we go. There is no escaping this phenomena because the human tribal instinct to be as good or better than everybody else and to be accepted in our society, forces us to participate. In addition, these are new ways for the marketing man to catch us – because they now 'buy' advertising space in the illusionary world of the computer game. So even the marketing man is being sold an illusion – a billboard in the land of illusion. Advertising billboards in a fake downtown city carries the same old messages and we subconsciously buy into the perception encoded and created. We are lying to ourselves in a world of lies and we only have ourselves to blame. We kill ourselves to afford to buy a product we don't need at an inflated price because of advertising costs of billboards in a land that doesn't exist. Stand back and think about how stupid this all is and then think about the eyes of a starving child. How does it make you feel?

Adults too are not immune to all of this. By extension there are now secondary worlds created on the world wide web of deceit, where we can recreate ourselves and live out a life of illusion so that we do not really have to face ourselves and our situations. We can truly offload all responsibility now and become another person as an extension of our worldly ego. Before we know it we die mentally and spiritually, let alone grow fat and insipid whilst glued to the VDU. In this created world we can even buy fake real estate using real hard earned money. We can then impress our real friends who join us within this unreal world as if we are really that fake creation by the extension of technology. Around us a million species die every year and awful suffering is in reality happening because we use energy to disappear into the dark worlds of desire.

And so technology, like everything else we humans create, is truly an extension of ourselves and it yet again is a world of falseness, covering up the real mess we are in. The truth is that the technology we created with all good intentions is now driving us and we have become extensions of the machine itself. A good example of this is the office. When I began my working life computers were not really useful, it took years for them to become useful and less expensive. Instead we shuffled paper and conversed with real humans face to face or over the telephone. It was, for all its faults, at least on a human level and at a human speed. But then things started to change and the invention of the facsimile machine altered things over night. Now people were distanced and instead of picking up the phone or popping into the office they simply faxed and hid behind the machine. The division of humanity was further increased by the one simple but imaginative machine. People knew that their fax had been delivered and the workload speeded up and more could be done. The fittest of the species now had to adapt to the machine. Suddenly the ordinary pace measured by human interaction and therefore based in a natural cycle was out of the window. And, because of competition, everybody got fax machines and everybody had to speed up in the same way that happened with the introduction of the telephone or the automated plough. The facsimile machine, in my mind, was a revolution, distancing man from each other and mechanizing him.

These leaps in technology are part and parcel of the human evolutionary cycle from the flint spear to the space shuttle. We cannot stop them, but we ought to be aware of their effects upon the human mind. Before we realized it, technology had transformed the office beyond all recognition with word processing, design and of course the internet and email. Everybody had to speed up again and now the truly successful alpha people multitask – using more than one technology at a time just to keep up and to stay alpha dominant and of course, to earn more of that illusionary money. The system is now beyond human-nature – we have created a monster, a Frankenstein, and we have lost ourselves. The lesson to learn is that just like the Frankenstein monster, it is a mirror of ourselves and it is destroying the very essence of what we are.

All of this is why even now in the 21st century we remain stupid humans who constantly battle with each other, because we are forcing ourselves away further and further from the truth of what we really are. We have created a world of imagination in which we can live out a dream life and to pay for it we live in hell.

Chapter 4

Food for Thought

One of the messages we seem to now be coming back to again and again is that we unknowingly and consistently delude ourselves. There are of course many reasons for this, but before we try to understand why, we need to take a look at one of the other delusional states of existence that we have created – food.

Food, at the end of the day, is sustenance for the physical body. We have evolved over millions of years perfectly well without the need to put chemicals in with our beef and yet this is precisely what we do today. But more than that, we also feed chemicals to the very livestock from which we derive beef. We are far removed in terms of food from our ancestors and it is in fact relatively recently that we have marched along this road of madness towards a world where we will be popping colored pills in replacement of good wholesome and natural food. In reality, due to the fact that our modern diets are so appalling and that processed food has basically next to no vitamins, minerals or proteins left, we actually stuff down our necks huge quantities of the same in tablet form.

Most of the problem can be traced back to the Second World War, when intense rationing hit Europe and indeed some form even in the USA. There simply was not enough to go around and many people became malnourished. But the people were rationed of ordinary foodstuffs, indicating that this was still a period of wholesome, home cooked food. I am still old enough myself to remember when mass processed freezer food began to be introduced and how every home had to have a freezer – thus contributing on a massive scale to global warming in one fell swoop.

Two things came out of the War in relation to food. The first one was clever invention. Because there was relatively little, we found new recipes and to feed the soldiers and the huddled masses, we started to pre-package food en masse. The second issue was the post war population boom. People needed to be put to work across Europe and infrastructures needed rebuilding. In the USA, the lack of destruction enabled them to grow at an exponential rate in comparison to war-torn Europe. For all of this and more, not least of which is the need for a future fighting force, people were encouraged to procreate – to make their nation the strongest and fittest should such conflicts occur again.

In the USA, where the infrastructure was intact and simply improved beyond all recognition, the population boomed, but more importantly, wealth grew like nowhere else. America grew, while Europe remade. America imagined a bright future, while Europe looked back afraid of the past – glaring at each other with afraid eyes. Invention fed necessity and from here on in the world began to taste the rewards of leisure time and breathe a sigh of relief – and who can blame them. But this leisure time developed into almost a commodity and soon it too became a battleground, with the opposing sides battling out over who had the biggest BBQ and who went where and how often on vacation. A new war was begun – time. To facilitate this, the masses were sold all-kinds of labor saving technologies and one of these was processed food and an incredible rise in take-away and fast-food restaurants. It was the beginning of the downfall of good natural and wholesome food.

In the beginning many of these fast-food restaurants provided good food, but eventually those with the lowest cost bases and most attractive and tasty food would succeed. To facilitate this cheapness, mass production needed to be undertaken of cattle and so vast swathes of land were cleared of trees without a thought to global warming and trees producing oxygen. Very little has changed and massive multi-billion-dollar corporations have been formed. In addition to this, new biological and chemical advancements brought new drugs, which meant that cattle could be force-grown. What resulted was slightly less tasty beef and so further chemicals were created to replace the taste, with added sugar and salt all making the final product taste like something it is in fact not. Today we consume thousands of times more sugar and salt than we should because it is added to our processed food for taste and preservation. One burger I recently had the disgust to eat out of pure starvation said that it had 40% of the recommended salt content. Add this to the fries and that is one lunch too many.

We also have the invention of new sodas, which are carbonated sugar and caffeine sources, leading to hyper-activity, followed by depression and addiction. In recent years there has been a public backlash against a lot of this and so the marketing men were called in to point out that a product, which in fact need not contain any fat at all, only contained 10% fat, as if this were now a healthy option.

We are now purposefully fed an overload of facts and figures – because it stops us even looking. We are told that a drink containing phenylketonurics ought to be good for us and actually help us to diet. In fact this simply means that it contains aspartame, an artificial sweetener that can cause toxic and poisonous side-effects. Aspartame dissolves in solution and is carried to all parts of the human body and has been known to cause blindness, tinnitus, epileptic seizures, memory loss and psychological problems. And yet we are fed this as a beneficial part of our diet to help us lose weight.

There would in fact, be no need for diet drinks, pills, packaged food and diet doctors if we ate good wholesome food and used our new leisure time to get out and about without the four-wheeled drive and leave the computer dream-world and TV behind. Our illusionary world is turning us into physical and psychical wrecks. But the marketing man, his junk food and his television technology forces us into a vicious cycle of eating to be happy because we are depressed that we cannot achieve what others have and perceive others to be happier than us and once we come down from the drug-laden food and drink we need another fix to avoid depression or anger.

Of course, an awful lot of our problems are caused by our own perceptions, or indeed those perceptions fostered for us. Take a recent trip I made to sunny California and Hollywood. I had never been before and my perceptions were of a massive film-set filled from head to foot in tight skinned immortal film-stars. I wasn't too disappointed because I did actually get to meet quite a few and what I found altered my own perceptions of the "rich and famous." I won't name anybody because that is personal and unfair, but I can say that I was extremely shocked to find stars whom I had previously assumed to be almost normal, snorting cocaine and smoking dope. As I learned more and more of this Hollywood lifestyle, I learned what a dog-eat-dog world they all live in and foster. Nothing there was as it seemed and yet it is sold to the world as a glitzy wonderful place full of beautiful rich people – a Barbie Heaven, when in fact it is a dark hell. The elderly fight off the signs of age with more and more surgery until their eyes pop out of the heads. The young males take so many hormone supplements that their manhood drops off as their muscles squash arteries and reduce life expectancy. The young females cut their bodies about until they have the perfect shape – albeit 90% plastic. And they all work day and night to afford their tippex teeth and rubber lips; and because of this they all need to take drugs to stay awake and fend of the impending depression caused by the drugs, food, lifestyle and lack of connection to nature. For every star we see in the sky there are hundreds of planets unseen and the same is true in Hollywood. For every star we see on our screens, who has managed to sleep with the right producer and overcome the physical abnormalities, there are thousands and thousands of wannabes serving coffee at some back street diner. Nothing wrong with serving coffee, as long as you know yourself and do not crucify yourself with desires for something you will probably never have. The trouble is, they all see themselves as the next Madonna or Tom Cruise – when in reality, one has to ask oneself, what did they do to get where they are now? And are they truly happy? How many people did they crush on the way up? And how much better is the world now for their efforts?

There are real stars walking on this planet and they are relatively unknown. They work hard in the background and have no desire to be "seen" or "known" by the whole world; people such as Bridget in Portugal who dedicated her entire life to saving stray animals and caring for the sick. She is a true star and yet she was always under-funded. She didn't care about her wrinkles, she cared about the puppy that had hours to live and held it in her arms until it died. She didn't worry about the latest overpriced dress from some French sounding designer who cannot decide whether he is a man or woman; she cared about the heat of the sun bearing down on starving stray dogs, kicked out of their homes and unloved.

Why do we revere these egotistical monsters in Hollywood and yet ignore the needy? We should all know the answer to this, and if we do not, then we need to reappraise our own lives.

However, even those with good intentions are not free of the marketing man as far as food is concerned. Many people recognize that the food fed to the masses is quite simply, junk, and so they seek out alternatives. In doing so they simply cannot avoid deception, which is formed at the heart of greed. For instance, to detoxify the body it is necessary to drink lots of water and yet our water supply is not always free of lime, fluoride and other natural and mankind introduced properties. To avoid this, the health conscious buy bottled water without considering the incredible effect this has on the environment with such small things as non-degradable plastic and the fuel cost of the transport. I recently totaled the miles our weekly shop had traveled to arrive in my house and found that we had bought products that could have circumnavigated the globe. Add to this the millions of people around the world doing the same and the transport and environmental cost is staggering.

In addition to this, everything was packaged in plastic and only 50% of it could be recycled. Of course in comparison relatively few people actually recycle and so the landfill sites around the world are pits of hell waiting for us to one day realize what we are creating. I wonder, will it all be too late by then and the world scrub us out like an irritating bug?

The same is true of most fast-food restaurants that cater for our insane 21st century dehumanized life. Your meal comes in plastic or polystyrene, your drink in a plastic and paper cup with a plastic straw and all of this with extra salt and sugar in plastic and paper bags. We only ever use these once and a standard family meal has huge amounts of packaging. All of this has utilized energy and chemicals in the making and all of it has already traveled thousands of miles to arrive in our bins. And further, all of this feeds our desire for more leisure time – speeding up the cooking and eating process so we can then do what? Use more energy and plastic products destroying the countryside? To pay for all of this, we have to work harder and harder and we pressurize each other in a million different ways. It is all, unnatural.

Sometimes, when you look at the system, you have to question whether the human race has gone mad. We know the world is warming and we know that we are causing most of it to exponentially increase, and yet we shrug our shoulders and feed the system.

There are many more techniques utilized by the marketing man to entice us into the system and feed us through like cattle. For instance some fast food restaurants actually have clever systems to maximize their profits. When the relatively slack times of the day come around, pleasant music and a warm atmosphere is in place to create an ambience people wish to remain in – the longer a person stays the more he spends on further drinks and possibly deserts. When the restaurant is busy, then cold air and loud music is used to get more people in and out of the premises – because more money is made from meal sales than just extra drinks and deserts. Before even this though, the smells of the food are blown out into the street to entice the senses into feelings of hunger. It is all one big cattle market, feeding cattle to cattle with caffeine laden addictive food packaged in plastic.

Plastic food eaten by plastic people in a world of plastic money.

Chapter 5

Madness

Because we live in a world of technology that dehumanizes us and we eat addictive food because of the inhuman state and speed of our existence, we end up with a confused mind. Our children are like sponges and so we have to question what we are teaching them? In addition to this, political correction has gone mad as we try to re-balance a world of insane effects our system is causing.

Today, children are being fed drugs by those doctors we are taught to trust because it speeds up the process of supposed mental correction and enables the drug companies to maximize profits and health officials to get more cattle through the surgery. Speed, profit and dehumanizing are the keys to the system we have created.

I personally know of children who are unbalanced because of everything we have been discussing so far and more. The parents no longer have the skills or time to bring up their own children because of work load and so they pay others to do it for them. They buy their children's love with computers and mobile phones and feed the growing child's sense of disassociation from their parents, society and their own humanity. The parents end up in a cycle of debt they cannot escape and in fact constantly re-feed the system of madness. The children have no idea what is happening to them and become depressed, hypersensitive and undisciplined. The answer is as ever, drugs. We pile all-manner of chemicals into our children, starting with the fast food and ending in the pharmaceutical giants drugs. What are we creating for the future of the world? We destroy the environment and now we even destroy the minds of our children.

The whole process is madness and simply feeds the profit of

corporations who cause the problem and then sell us the cure.

And yet, we cannot be absolved of responsibility, no matter how hard we try. We have only ourselves to blame because we ought to know better. Adults have the freewill to learn and gather this knowledge and yet we would rather spend our hard earned money gambling, buying more drugs in the form of alcohol, cigarettes and even illegal substances and desperately trying to liven up our dull lives with extreme sports or watching the stars parade on television. We prefer to pay thousands in loans to get a huge four-by-four, which destroys the environment and places us deeper into the cycle of debt like a hamster on a wheel. And yet none of it satisfies us and we ourselves fall into depression, which requires more spending and more drugs. We visit psychologists, priests and buy all-kinds of products to make us feel better and yet never manage to discover the secret formula for our own happiness. The confused web we spin around ourselves clouds the fact that our happiness will only be found in simplicity – from where we came. Instead, we act like spoilt brats and never grow, learn or mature. Our children copy and we increase the depression and problems of the world and we call it freedom. True freedom is knowledge of this state we are in and an understanding that we do not need to partake of this food of evil.

The human dilemma of imbalance is not new. It is in fact as old as man. The problem today is that the majority of the globe has forgotten or been led to forget the simple methods of coming to terms with this duality and correcting it. To fully understand it we have to go right back to the start and we may have to get a little metaphysical.

In the beginning was the big bang. The One divided and divided and spewed outwards into chaos. A vast unimaginable chaotic mess of division started the whole process. In time all this division began to come back together and form into order.

Eventually out of this new found relative order life emerged. Life emerged from the original One, but it could only form where there was the universal special element of gravity in perfect balance. Gravity on Earth runs around the center of the planet as it does on all planets. This underlying law of the universe reveals the driving force of all order/chaos patterns – that it must return to the One from where it came. As conscious beings we feel this intense pull upon our very soul and realize that we are ourselves divided – we mirror the order and chaos of the universe itself. It is seen in our physical forms as we unite with the opposite sex and reconnect. This is the driving force of the entire universe and the truth of it is revealed when one understands that the universe itself will one day be drawn back into the One via the big crunch. The amazing metaphysical concept of all of this is that we can and have become conscious of the drive of the universe itself – we have become aware of god. The reason for this is very simple, because we ourselves are mirrors of this natural universe because we are in it and of it. We are mini-universes ourselves and we express this concept in our own nature. The trouble is that we as relatively recently conscious beings in this universe are like new-born stars – still in the chaotic state. We have to grow and form and mature in-order to be balanced and ordered. At the moment we are causing chaos with everything we do, with very few people understanding that their delusional state is actually delusional at all, and without understanding there can be no correction.

Professor James Gardner, a peer reviewed philosopher of universal law said in *What is Enlightenment* magazine that the universe is intelligent at the subatomic level and that it acts like a DNA feedback loop. DNA, as it instructs cells to grow is fed back information by the cell at the quantum level and it then uses this information and sends back further instructions. It is believed that the universe does this also and that we are part of the cellular structure feeding information back into the universal DNA and then receiving new instructions. We are all connected to every-thing via quantum particle entanglement – we just don't know it. We are in fact conscious beings at a level of existence that is mathematically in perfect balance with the universe and we are at the very center of this structure. There are as many atoms within us as there are stars in the universe – we are perfectly centered in the greater cosmic soup. In fact it would take as many humans to make the mass of our very own sun, as there are atoms within us – and so we are at the very center of our solar system. We are connected perfectly to the universe both at the quantum level and the mathematical harmonious level – it is perfection created from chaos.

When our ancestors blew off their conscious world and entered altered states they uncovered this connection and understood. They left this information for us in symbols and texts, but because the experience is so ineffable we fail to understand what they were saying. In addition to this those humans who had created a massive power base with religion did not want their business undermining and so clamped down on anybody who revealed the inner wisdom of connection to the divine in the self or Gnosis. In this way the advancement of understanding was held back and division has ever since grown in the mind of man.

Today we have a divided world created by the divided mind of man, which simply wishes to go back to the One. It is consciousness arguing with the unconscious world that is causing this division – for the facts speak for themselves. We are not separate from the universe in which we reside, we are in fact at the mid-point of it all and we are conscious of it. The depth of this is incredible, for it is at the mid-point between awake and asleep that man enters into an altered state of consciousness and emerges with intense concepts of knowledge. Our mind mirrors the mind of the universe and we are physically at the very center.

However, there have been a great many men and women

throughout time who have managed to get the message across and it can be found hidden within religious texts, which were then literalism and utilized by the power bases, so that they eventually lost all meaning.

The truth is that we can help our own madness and that we do not require drugs or priests to do so. All we need is *strength, will* and *knowledge*. We can take these three words and use them to better ourselves by seeking balance in our lives. We are all positive and negative and we constantly cycle between them. The true understanding will only be found in the point between these cycles – in a neutral state and it is in this state that people find greater understanding, artistic expression and calm. How do we do this? It is simple and yet seemingly a million miles away from where we are. Every element of your past needs to be understood to be in the past. It is not with you now, unless you make it so. The future too need not be worried about, for worry causes conflict and chaos and tips the balance. Both the past and the future are poles and if we live in either then we are again dividing our mind. To live now is an anagram of own and it is time that we owned our own lives and stopped shuffling responsibility for ourselves, beliefs, actions etc on other times – let alone people, states and religions. The time and place now is the space between past and future and so time itself reveals the truths of gravity and number linked to our own well-being.

This balancing of the extremes and finding the place between is multi-leveled and works on all things in our lives. If we all applied this balance then we would all be happier and more content – but we would have to apply it to every level of our lives. This, like gravity, would affect those people around us and cause a more balanced society (minor or major). So too if we are chaotic and unbalanced (like for instance Adolf Hitler) then we would cause more division in others. Influence is itself a good benchmark – how are we influencing others?

We can cause all-kinds of cycles around us, from influencing a cycle in our children with simple things like swearing, to influencing them with love, balanced with discipline. And this brings us full circle to our children and feeding them drugs because we and the chaotic world around them has set them on a treadmill of imbalance. They need to know that we love them enough to keep them safe. It's like putting them into a small field when they are small, with a safety fence all around. As they grow, we simply move the fence outwards and make the field larger – we expand their horizons, but still within a safety net. This allows growth, but in a loving and balanced way. Too small a field will restrict growth and they will learn little and this is where we get overbearing and overprotective parents. If we fail to place a fence around the field at all then we have children who unconsciously think that they are unloved and this shadow in the mind will one day emerge. We will see our children running off over into other fields, causing chaos with others and placing themselves in physical and psychological danger. They will run into the unknown (for them) and before long will land up in trouble that they have not been prepared for. We will then have to go to extreme lengths to bring them back – if indeed we even notice. All of this is true for society at large too.

Francis Bacon, the 16th century writer and once Lord Chancellor of England, said in his essay *Of Goodness and Goodness of Nature*:

"Sell all thou hast, and give it to the poor, and follow me; but sell not all thou hast, except thou come and follow me; that is, except thou have a vocation wherein thou mayest do as much good with little means as with great; for otherwise in feeding the streams thou driest the fountain."

Bacon is showing that no matter how good your intentions may be, if you have not the right knowledge, then you will be like a dry fountain – useless. We must show willing to improve, but begin in small ways and improve ourselves first before attempting to infect others.

You see, we are really all to blame for the state of affairs. For the environment; for feeding anti-depressant drugs to children; for our own psychosis. Each one of us knowingly uses other people to feed our own self propelled delusional state. For instance we all know beyond all doubt that Hollywood stars are ordinary human beings and yet we also know that the majority of them are not happy. I recently spent a week with one of Hollywood's top producers who used to work in the business of films. The tales that man has to tell about the rich and famous, whom the masses idolize, are incredible. It's like worshipping god, knowing that he regularly injects heroin.

There is one particular tale that I found most interesting and enlightening. One day the producer in question turned up to work at the studio and went about his daily business. He went down to the recording studio where there were other people with whom he worked. On the couch was a young man who was a friend of a member of staff. The producer went up to the man because he looked depressed and he discovered that he had been kicked out of his apartment, was drugged and had nowhere to go. This kind of story is very common in Hollywood and indeed many other such places of deity worship, however the difference here is that years later the man on the couch would become one of the world's biggest big screen stars and comedian actors.

The actor in question had slipped into a cycle of the system and had no idea he was in it – he was not self aware and had no idea that he was in the cycle. He was depressed because his delusional state – i.e. the dream world of Hollywood – had not come true. But this kind of story fuels the abortion that truly is the god and devil making machine called Hollywood. People see these ordinary down and out characters and truly believe they too can succeed and live in a delusional world. All that happens is that people romantically assume that they will be spotted for their immense talent and that they will be catapulted to fame and fortune overnight. It almost never happens that way. Instead people arrive in droves to become gods and goddesses based upon lies and deceit and end up as part of yet another meat factory. Drink, drugs and debt are more often than not the only outcome. Suicide rates increase; children are brought up in the most insane delusional and illusionary world outside of the Vatican and the cycle repeats. Out of every star who supposedly makes it big time there are not hundreds, not thousands, but millions of people who struggle to pay their rent whilst serving coffee at Denny's. But these millions delude themselves with the dream of the few and in this they lose themselves.

There are two levels of traps into this world. The first one is the assumption that the characters that actors portray on screen are real. We see what they do and believe in them. When Pierce Brosnan played James Bond he was acting the part. He is nothing at all like that fictional character in real life. It is all illusion. Men around the world watched him and tried to emulate him, as Bond. This is why secondary selling is so productive. This is where we are sold items or symbols from the film, so that we can pretend to be the person seen. For instance we may go and buy a Bond-type car, or even more delusional, we may buy the computer game and disappear into the world of espionage (which never has and never will be anything like James Bond). All of this feeds yet further the world of illusion and we buy into it hook, line and sinker. We all do this in one way or another. It may not necessarily be a film or TV show that we emulate, it may be a character from a book, or somebody that has influenced us in the past. Either way, it is yet still further distancing us from our self.

The second tier of entry is that we believe the stars to be extra-special people. We see them in magazines and on the TV and believe the painted images actually portray the real person. We listen to the carefully orchestrated words and read the publicist's lies and assume everything is just perfect at the top. It has been this way ever since Pharaoh had hieroglyphs carved into rock. There are techniques used to create this aura of perfection. Language is used such as *alliteration, repetition* and *rhetorical questions*. "Is Pierce Brosnan a real life James Bond?" This is a rhetorical question that seeps into the subconscious mind and places a concept there to gently settle. Newspapers, news shows, radio, magazines and now the internet are all utilized in this way and we don't even realize that we are being lead down a certain path. For instance, most countries have a dualistic press. One side will veer towards the left and the others towards the right. The same story will be reported in two completely different ways. "Is President XXX going too far?" Would be a rhetorical question implying that the president is going too far, whereas "Our President Stands Firm" implies quite the opposite and personalizes him with "our." The same thing is reported, but different angles used and so the reading public (and indeed viewing public) are swayed and split. There is almost no unbiased reporting, because even the reporter has his own opinion (subjective) and it is in the same way impossible for any of us not to have an opinion and thereby be objective, and to read into the story something which may not even be there. This simple example follows through in all our daily lives and we are completely unconscious of it. In fact we naturally do it in conversation with each other, to give strength to our arguments.

Both of these traps into the ultimate delusional world of Hollywood (and everything from there downwards) are the same. They are both based upon an illusion and a delusion. Hollywood creates the illusion and we want to believe it to somehow make the world seem right and hence the delusion sets in. We are very much prone to ignore and sideline bad news (personal) unless it gives us esteem (talking point based upon superior knowledge). We hope for the best (for ourselves and loved ones) and are willing to trust our deluded senses over our intuition, which itself is ostracized into the unconscious world. It cannot all be a lie? (Can it?) The fact is, behind every person, whether rich or poor, there is a divided human being and one that is nothing to worship, as we seem to the Hollywood set. Our fascination with Hollywood is more often than not due to our own shortcomings.

Chapter 6

Internet Enlightenment

Almost everybody who reads this book will have been on, or seen the internet world. It is like escaping the body and somehow jumping into another dimension. We stare like zombies into a world that can offer us anything we want. From buying almost anything, even sex, to showing ourselves off and emulating the stars. With the internet we can do it all. But I believe it to be a dangerous world for the mind of man.

The word *man* is derived from *mind* and this was the concept of man himself – that he was seen not as the sum of his parts, but as the thinking processor unit behind the eyes. He was more than his legs and arms, for when they ceased to function the mind remained. It was the very thing that set him apart from the other living breathing beings on our planet (so we believe). Man realized he was alive; he realized that he existed, had joy, worry, fear. He began to set the world in-order and suddenly the planet and the universe itself existed, because we conceived of it. This separated us from the rest, not just in terms of how we thought, but we even physically began to lose our connection. The anxious element of this situation gave us responsibility for our selves and ever since this fear emerged man attempted to replace it with the concepts of deities – an attempt to remove responsibility for our actions and indeed our thoughts. We were so thankful for this weight off our shoulders that the religious authorities grew at an alarming rate, utilizing this fear against us and growing some more. Even now in the 21st century all our sins can be taken away by the savior gods. These sins are caused by the parts of the mind that shadow us – the other side that we mostly attempt to ignore. Yes, all of us do this, we all claim to be better than that! But it was not so long ago that whole nations were swayed into the land of shadows by a charismatic leader who drew around him mini-demons and set the world on a path of hellish destruction.

Nazi Germany was created by and from the mind of man – namely Adolf Hitler. This one divided and neurotic individual gathered the knowledge on how to 'convince' people of his outlook. All the tools Hitler and his cohorts used are exactly the same as those we have been discussing throughout this book. The German people were not evil, they were human and they were guided on a path by the shadow of another. Their evil sides were drawn out in the name of good and righteousness and in the end nobody knew that what they were doing was evil itself because they had forgotten themselves entirely. All judgement and responsibility had been taken away from them in the name of the State and because humans enjoy losing this responsibility they were a happy people. Because of this happiness, this bliss in darkness, they could simply not understand why other nations did not want to join them. There is absolutely nothing new here at all – this is a constant cyclic human pattern that has occurred for millennia and occurs everyday in everybody's life. We all tip out of balance in many ways and in many subjects. Let's have a look at a specific pattern and subject that is relevant today because of the growing surge in its popularity – the enlightenment.

Enlightenment is knowledge gained and understood at a deep level of reality. It is a moment of pure insight and understanding that resonates with our most inner mind and links to that thing I call the intuition. We all have moments of enlightenment, when we supposedly suddenly realize a truth. The fact is, that like the stars of Hollywood, nothing happens overnight and enlightenment's do not happen overnight. Instead they are *convergences* of *knowledge* fusing in the *mind* at one point in *time* and releasing *understanding* back into the *mind*. If we comprehend the truth behind this simple sentence then we truly understand what enlightenment is. Let's break it down for those of us that do not get it just yet:

> The convergence of knowledge. Well quite simply we all learn every moment of the day, we just may not always be aware of this learning process (i.e. conscious understanding). Over the course of our lives we learn a great many things and occasionally and often by pure accident things we have learned meet and make sense. The moment we find the last piece of the jigsaw puzzle we suddenly see the whole picture – whereas before that we knew each part mattered, we just didn't know how or why. All of this occurs in the *mind*, which then tells itself that it has understood and releases pleasure center hormones as a gift for making the breakthrough. We experience this *feeling*, which adds weight and power to the emotion of the enlightenment experience.

Now this is where the problem or duality of this experience can be found, for the emotional reaction caused gives the individual a sense of it being profoundly true and that the world ought to revolve around it. The *experience* gains more credit because of *feeling* than the actual knowledge gained. There are a great many experienced mystics from a range of religions that have all had the enlightenment experience and yet they cannot all be right for they come from diametrically opposed corners of the theoretical spectrum. It is therefore a personal experience, for the individual and yet has repercussions upon all those around it.

One of the experiences that has caused more dangerous reactions is the blinding flash. This is something I have written on extensively and yet the point needs to be reiterated that it causes division and severe mental problems. This blinding flash in the mind is the result of an electromagnetic, chemical and biological reaction via the nervous system into the brain, releasing pleasure hormones and a sense of knowledge due to the sudden connectivity of all parts of the neural network at one moment in time.

There may indeed be a deeper connection to a quantum under-standing at an archetypal level involved, however this does not discount the problem with this experience – that it can and does cause the individual to lose all sense of reality (whatever that may mean). Due to the fact that this is an emotional state it causes an imbalance in the emotional state and because it is a sudden physical reaction (chemical/biological) then there is no understanding of what it is and so the imagination fills in the gaps with deities and all-manner of other weird and wonderful things. I do not speak from a position of ignorance, I know what reactions have been caused by this experience and how it has sadly affected perfectly ordinary people and ruined their (and others) lives. I will give one true example, on the understanding that I have in fact seen this exact same thing now hundreds of times.

Following the launch of my book *Gnosis: The Secret of Solomon's Temple Revealed*, which speaks of this experience and it's relationship to the symbols of the Bible and other religious texts, I was contacted by an individual who at first thanked me profusely for the book. I responded as any decent author would with a thank you note and my best wishes. The correspondent then followed up with a statement that he would like to explain his personal experience to me in the hope that I might have some insight. I duly responded that I would take a look and see if there was anything I could add. A small snippet of the experience came back, from which I could derive very little and I was then told that this was a teaser and that if I wanted to know the real truth of the experience then we would have to meet. I then decided to back down, sensing an imbalance in the individual that I recognized from previous exchanges with other individuals – the pattern was the same. The way I backed down was by refusing to accept that I would have to keep such a great and wonderful thing from mankind, as the individual in question wanted me to keep it secret. I actually have a problem with secrecy when it is not required. Truth is truth for all mankind to decide upon and if he wanted it kept a secret, then I humbly said that I simply couldn't meet up and waste his time. What do you think the individual did? Sent me diatribe after diatribe of verbal abuse, calling me every name I know and some more. Of course, having had this numerous times I knew this was going to be the reaction, but tried my best in love, compassion and in balance to back out. The problem is that too many reactions like this can cause people like me, authors etc, to never answer correspondence and to never trust in humanity again. I, however, refuse to do that and still answer my mail. I know myself and therefore am not joined at the hip with such notions of others.

The point of the tale is this: did this experience balance this individual? Did it give him a truer sense of perspective? Has it truly enlightened him? If this experience was truly the enlightenment, then I myself need to re-appraise the meaning of the word, for it certainly does not seem to me that the individual had emerged a better person. In fact, out of all the people I have met who have had this particular blinding flash experience that some call the Kundalini, I have yet to meet one I deem perfectly balanced. Most of them (that I have met) can tip out of balance instantly and cause chaos almost everywhere. Strive not for the light, but for wisdom. True wisdom does not force you into a violent rage when somebody does not agree with you. This emotional experience, for that is what it is, brings on a religious experience and we all know how this can in fact force us to lose ourselves in the process. The intense sense of knowing, claimed by the one experiencing the emotional state, brings a sense of deluded euphoria and false sense of self worth – I am more holy than thou! Others, who have not therefore experienced the emotional state are less holy and therefore know nothing. The world must then revolve around this individual and all those who come into contact with them will be tossed around by the maelstrom of the chaotic individual – just like the whirlwind of abuse I am sometimes pulled into. Because of the arrogance and confidence of the individual, those in society who are looking for somebody to take away their responsibilities, are drawn to these people as beacons of light, as saviors. They succeed because they have an answer. It may not be the answer, but at least it is an answer – and a pretty exciting one at that.

All of that said, the person who can enter into this state of being in balance and in knowledge of the self may very well be accessing an archetypal world of truth – the state of Oneness. But these individuals are extremely rare and the society in which we live does not allow the mind to be free enough nor give it sufficient time to truly be in such a balanced state. It will not come to those that strive, but to those that wait and ponder. There is more to our existence, but if that supposed knowledge causes you to be a chaotic influence amongst others then it is not wisdom and it is not the true self.

Today, all-manner of weird and wonderful new religions are in fact emerging. It has always been the case that new religions emerge with each new generation, but normally this has been tempered by State and the existing power religion, as well as the speed of communication and travel. Now most of these barriers are seemingly being sidelined by the internet.

In the same way that an original leader, mystic or prophet of the past would spread the word of his or her supposed enlightenment, today the individual prophets of the world have a unique outlet. They no longer have to meet other folks at the market or outside the Temple walls. They no longer have to gather forces in localized towns and villages and ask apostles to spread the word. Today they can forge ahead and spread their word via websites, articles and email shots. One particular group even took my name and made up a whole host of things I said and posted these comments all over the net. I simply don't have time or will power to follow their nonsense.

PC proselytizing is the new religion and in this way there is something for everyone. Every emotional experience that is driven by every individual life and hormone is spread across the world and so there are now millions of religions. These include alien worship (in many guises), clairvoyance, spiritualism, strands of older religions and the more literal goddess and god worship of personality. There may be some truth in some of these, there may not, but evidence seems to now be subjective, unchecked and certainly of a personal experience in nature. We trust in what we read and see. We read the experience of an individual on a website and what reason do we have to doubt them? But do we know them? Can we really trust them? We have to remind ourselves of Adolf Hitler. We have to know who we are ourselves before we have the ability to know another properly.

On top of all this emotional and spiritual illusion being spread around the world like never before, we also have the predators of the greed system. Many of us are innocently looking through the net, searching for something that interests us. We are all familiar with the now infamous pop-up system, whereby we go to a particular website because we have been led there from a search engine and advertisements pop up to annoy us. For me this has the opposite effect that the advertiser probably wanted, but then I am not somebody who succumbs to advertising easily anyway. But there is a more insidious form of getting our money, from illegal and false websites that sell us something, ask us for credit card details and then we never receive the goods. Meanwhile our cards have been completely stripped of all data and money. On top of this we now have spam (email junk mail) selling us everything from viagra to real estate, but worse still there is spam that tries to yet again strip us of our hard earned cash in return for nothing. Below are a few examples of the madness of man and remember that these things wouldn't and couldn't be done if it were firstly not possible, but secondly, if people weren't gullible enough to actually complete the forms and hand over their money. Notice how bad the English and grammar is which gives us a clue to the fact that these are either written and sent from outside of the English speaking world or that they are meant to look that way.

I agreed to pay the amount you want as buy it now and any additional money for the shipping. But I am using this opportunity to inform you that the amount that will be on the money order will more than your item fees. I don't really know the exact amount it will be.

Because it will be issue by my client, the reason of the over payment is that the amount on the money order has been signed, and it is more than your item fees. So once you receive it, you must deduct ur item fees and Western Union the balance money to my client manager in Africa, and the item is going to Africa.

There will be no problem about the shipment. I want you to responsible for it. Also make sure you deduct your item fees and western union any aditional money on the m/o once you receive it. Here we go i would have end the auction but i don't know how to do it. So I want you to go and end the auction for me asap to assure you that i am really interested in your item. I will add extra $5.00 in your payment if you end the auction for me asap. And email me your phone# and where the money order will be addressed to asap today.

Below are the questions i have for you?

1) *Is the item in good condition?*
2) *Is any westernunion location where you will be able to send the balance money around you?*
3) *Can you make sure you get the m/o cash at ur bank the sameday you receive it?*
4) *Can you allow me to send DHL for the pick up and complete the transaction the day you receive the moneyorder?*

If yes too all my questions. Kindly email me back asap today so that the

moneyorder can be send asap.
Thanks.

Dear Friend
My name is Larry Douglas-West; I represent a group of senators. We need the assistance of a reliable and trustworthy person/Business firm to help receive money for investments overseas on their behalf. The money has been deposited with a security firm. If you are willing to be our partner, send your name, telephone & fax Numbers, postal & office address and email address to my email: xx@xx, so that we will be able to get across to you. Further details will be discussed as soon as we receive your confirmation of interest. We shall make available you all relevant documents of the fund deposit with the security firm. For helping in receiving the funds and investing into either real estate, buying stocks/share, and going into a joint venture with you and your associates, you will receive 25% of the $150 million. As soon as you indicate your Interest, further details will be discussed on the procedure that we will follow in accomplishing this deal. Regards, Larry Douglas-West

A benefactor has mandated me to get someone that can assist her and her family in retrieving her package containing some amount of money from a Security Company in Europe. The benefactor and her children have been confined only to their country home and all their calls and movements are monitored, as a result, it's absolutely impossible for them to do anything as regards retrieving the money. Their only means of communication is via Internet and you are being contacted because your assistance is needed in claiming the funds on their behalf. The amount was accrued from Diamond sales over a period of ten years and its 85M Pounds (Eight-Five Million Pounds). These funds are fully free of any liens, or encumbrances and are clean, clear and have no criminal origin. The funds have nothing to do with any form of illegality and all documentations needed to prove the source of the funds were submitted when the funds were being deposited and these documents would prove the source of the funds and authenticate the fact that the funds are clean and has no links whatsoever with either drugs or terrorism. For your assistance in this transaction, the benefactor and her Children have agreed to give you 50% of the total amount of money which is equivalent to 42,500,000M Pounds (Forty-Two Million, Five hundred and Fifty Thousand, Pounds) and this role simply entails retrieving the funds on their behalf from the Diplomats in America and all the information needed to claim the funds would be sent to you as soon as you indicate your interest in assisting them as well as providing the following information to facilitate The smooth conclusion of the transaction.

1) Your Full Name: _____

2) Your Address: _____

3) Your Telephone Number: _____

4) Your Fax Number: _____

5) Your Mobile Number: _____

6) The Name of the Closest Airport to your City of
  Residence:_____

7) Your Age_____

8) Your Occupation_____

9)Your I.D_____

I await your response urgently.

Dr. Phil Kelley

Following the ongoing investigations by the Economic and Financial Crimes Commission and the recent statement by the commission that 31 states are under investigation, my Boss has directed me to seek a foreigner to work with us and safe-keep his money that is currently in London.

This move is necessary because the commission will confiscate the money if they get to it. This is why my Boss is worried and has asked me to immediately locate a foreign individual that can be trusted to receive this money and keep it safe. Though the money was not deposited in his name, we still thought it wise to move the money from its present location. This is why you are needed and you will be handsomely rewarded once we successfully get this money under your care. Please respond immediately and provide me with your contact information and mailing address. Once we get acquainted, I will give you all the information about the deposit and how you are to get it. Note that you are to deal directly with me as the name and identity of my Boss will not be disclosed to avoid jeopardizing this business. He is a sitting Governor of one of the states here in Nigeria and will be leaving office by May 2007. Your urgent response is required please. Reply through this email address: c.udeh@yahoo.com. My direct line is 234 803 332 1710, call me anytime of the day.

Yours truly,

Charles Udeh

My Dear Friend

I'm happy to inform you about my success in getting those funds transferred under the cooperation of a new partner from Turkey. Presently I m in Turkey for investment projects with my own share of the total Contract sum. Mean while, I didn't forget your past efforts and attempts to assist me in transferring those funds despite that it failed us some How. Now contact my secretary in Accra Ghana West Africa her information below:

Name Mrs. Rosemarry James

E-mail

Tel: +233 242 874612

Ask her to send you the Draft what of US$950.000.00 (NINE HUNDRED AND FIFTY THOUSAND UNITED STATE DOLLAR) which i kept for your compensation for all your past efforts and attempts to assist me in this matter. I appreciated your efforts at that time very much, so feel free and get in touched with my secretary Mrs. Rosemarry James and instruct her where to send the Draft to you.

Please do let me know immediately you receive it so that we can share the joy after all the sufferness at that time. in this moment, I m very busy here because of the investment projects which me and my new partner are having at hand, finally, remember that i had forwarded instruction to my secretary on your behalf to receive the Draft, so feel free to forward all your information to Mrs. Rosemarry James and where to send the Draft to smoothly and I assure you she will do as you said if only you follow her advise.

With best regards,

Mr. Nannan John Kwame.

N.B Please i may not respond to your email due to i am very busy here in Turkey.

The National Lottery Committee

P O Box 1010 Liverpool,

 L70 1NL UNITED KINGDOM

(Customer Services)

Dear Customer,

We are obliged to inform you that we have succeeded in resolving all related problems that has held the transfer impossible. With the help of the International Monetary Fund(IMF) who have rendered a tremendous help to this Exercise. We regret to announce the misman agement of beneficiaries fund by our appointed zonal managers; we are not able to meet up with the winner's amount due to the list of names that are due for payment.

In appreciation of your patients and understanding to receive your fund we have decided to compensate you with the sum of ($950,000.00) Bank Draft. Your identification code IS UKTNL5623 for compensation. You are to contact our coordinator officer Mr.David Green, Access management and support initiatives, a consultant firm on e-mail address: amsi.consultant@yahoo.dk

Please do send him your:- (1)FULL NAMES: (2)CONTACT

ADDRESS: (3)E-MAIL ADDRESS: (4)AGE & SEX: (5) TELEPHONE NUMBER: (6)FAX NUMBER: (7)COUNTRY OF ORIGIN: (8)STATE OF ORIGIN: (9)BREIF DESCRIPTION OF YOUR COMPANY.

Do not hesitate to let us know immediately you receive your fund so that we can take account of how many beneficiaries were paid.

Johnson Anthony
NATIONAL COORDINATOR
LIVERPOOL LONDO.

Someone is wating to sleep with you.
View the largest database of singles in the world.
Browse the revealing photo profiles now.

So far so good, I am very happy to inform you about my success in getting those funds transferred under the cooperation of a new partner from Hong Kong.

Presently I'm in India for investment projects with my own share of the total sum. Meanwhile,I didn't forget your past efforts and attempts to assist me in transferring those funds despite that it failed us some how.

In appreciation of your assistance I have mapped out as a compen-sation and wrote on your favour a check worth of Us$1.6m. So, you can now contact my secretary in Benin republic, Mr John Bonyi on his e-mail address (mrbonyi145@yahoo.it) and phone number + 22997020406 ask him to send you the total of Us$1.6m. which I kept for your compensation for all the past efforts and attempts to assist me in this matter.

Bear in mind that this Us$1.6m. is in draft, not cash, so you need to send to him your full names and address as where this draft/check will be posted/delivered.

I appreciated your efforts at that time very much. So feel free to get in touched with my secretary Mr.John Bonyi and furnish him with the below information to enable him send the Bank Draft to you at your own expense as I have done enough by allocating such huge amount to you.

Even my current partner is not happy that i have to allocate such amount to you bearing in mind your nonchalant attitude to the transaction at its crucial stage.

And make sure that you furnish him with the following information:

Your full name:

Contact and mailing address:

Telephone and cellphone numbers:

Cell:

In the moment, I'm very busy here because of the investment projects which me and the new partner are having at hand. Finally, bear in mind that I had forwarded instruction to my secretary to mail the draft to you once receipt of the above information. Regards,

Mr. Koku Tofa

As can be seen from the forgoing, mankind is still ingenious and still grappling with each other to make money. However, its does reveal the other shadow side of our human nature – that we will often turn to almost anything to better our own lives. The people sending out these emails probably have a family, wife, children, friends and they may even go to church on Sundays. They may be sitting in some Third World room trying to get money from us rich Westerners, or they may be already rich themselves and sat in a plush office somewhere. Whatever the truth – they have turned their conscience off like a light bulb and have split their ideas of right and wrong according to their own needs or desires. It is such an easy step for many people. I remember in the 1980's in the UK seeing battles in the streets between ordinary working miners and policemen. On one side of my family were policemen and on the other miners. Ordinarily they met up down at the pub or saw each other at family social gatherings. But in the 1980's

State and Union collided and sides were taken and battles fought. Ordinary folk fought for another's ideal. Family members turned on each other instantly, beating each other to a pulp and leaving them for dead. There were scenes reminiscent of the Eastern block or even dare I say it, Nazi Germany. The German people are not all a special race geared towards world domination and policemen are not all dominating control freaks. All of mankind is capable of the worst atrocities and all mankind is capable of the greatest good. We are two in one, divided and confused. But when we come together we can be very bad or very good. We can rise as nations or societies and manifest everyman's duality on a massive scale. This is why too much power in the hands of one man is dangerous, because it is not tempered by extra minds and so like Stalin, Hitler and a whole host of other dictators from the past, the many can fall under the magic of the one and be destroyed by the one. In the 1980's many in England were under the gaze and mesmerized by Prime Minister Thatcher with her steely ways. The nation divided, and balance for a moment was lost. In that situation, one side or another had to win, for no middle ground was available due to the power of the PM.

Today, we at least have the numbers on the internet to balance out any dictatorial element, but the power of the few naturally emerges from the mire and we have major corporations controlling much of what we see – even if it is all an illusion. Google, Yahoo and other search engines choose via computer programs which websites get listed and I know several people who have complained to me that their site was banned for one reason or another, and so, the true freedom we expect and perceive with the www is not actually there. One site was removed from Google I am told, because it had an upturned cross as the logo and may have caused offence.

Wherever man finds a market place; wherever he sets up a stall, then lies and deceit quickly follow, because it is within our nature and the sooner each one of us realizes that we have a shadow side, the better we will be to deal with it. The State reacts like a larger version of ourselves and will jump on lies and deceit where found or highlighted and so more and more State control is the result. And because the State is a larger version of ourselves, it too has a shadow side and it too uses lies and deceit. Why therefore would anybody hand over the responsibility, respect and life to State or Religion, when they are manifestations of the divided mind of man? Don't.

Chapter 7

Dumbing Down

To dumb down is quite simply to treat people as if they were dumb, and this is a big issue in the world today. Let me give you an example. On a breakfast show on TV recently there was a story run about James Bond in-order to promote the latest film. A competition was announced to win holidays in some far off exotic location. This was an obvious advertisement for the holiday company promoting its Bond-style holidays and also for the film itself. Everybody jumps on the band-wagon when something big like this happens and so the normal chat-room style element of the breakfast show was used to get at the people at home on a cold winters morning in the UK who were all about to trudge off to work. The idea of a Bond (and hence attachment of the self to this concept) and the warm sunny climes was an obvious diversionary tactic to pull upon the inner desires of people. Now of course this isn't dumb, it's very clever on the part of the marketing man and the networking and gelling of the various media and organizations to enable this feat of mental manipulation.

In fact the dumb element and in my opinion the insulting part came when they gave the question: What is the code of James Bond? Well, if you had been on Mars for the past 50 years I could understand you not knowing the number immediately, but to help all the aliens along they gave us three options:

Was it A) 007 B) 006 or C) 005? Well, do you know the answer? Well if you do then you could call a phone number in your excitement and spend £1 (about $2 then) making the call, leaving your name, address and email with a machine which then takes that information and uses it by selling it to other marketing companies for mail-shots and all-manner of things. Of course the truth of this is that it is a wonderfully ingenious money-making scheme. The holiday costs around £3000 and yet sells for around £10000 and so we appear to win a holiday worth £10000! Hundreds of thousands of people jump up off their couches and dial (if indeed the phone isn't a wireless version that rests permanently beside them along with their mobile phone, DVD remote, TV remote, VHS remote and of course the cable remote.) Each call sells at £1, making hundreds of thousands of pounds. The holiday company gets free advertising, Bond gets free advertising, the marketing companies sell on the data and the TV station makes a huge profit.

The question is purposefully simple, so that people rush around making calls, spending huge amounts of money. This happens every single day of the year, several times a day. Imagine how much money is being made from stupidly simple competitions like this. Imagine what we could do with such money - like help to save dying species for instance. Instead we hand over our brains and our money to this lowest of rubbish and feed further the machine that dreamt it up.

This little tale is a prime example of what is occurring in the world of the media. It is not just within the realms of television, this occurs too on radio, in magazines, on the internet and in direct sales efforts such as telesales and direct mail. We are all constantly bombarded with this inept nonsense. We no longer have to think too hard, because all the work is being done for us. The answers to quizzes are easy, the traps set and the gullible beguiled. It seems everybody and everything in the public gaze is now succumbing to these methods. Even our politicians speak to the masses as if they are stupid and we only have ourselves to blame. You see there is a reason for all this and it may be driven by greed, but it is used because of one thing.

The Lowest Common Denominator

Because all these simple systems work on the majority of people, from young to old, then the rest of us have to put up with it. This is *the lowest common denominator*. For instance we all have to put up with the government that democracy says via votes is the popular choice. The votes are being cast by the same people who rush to their phones and spend millions in the example above. Is this an intellectual decision? Are we truly getting the government that is best for us? Or are we getting the government that has proven to be the best at spinning a dumbed down message to the masses? I know I am being very naughty here and I will leave that political thought to the reader, suffice to say democracy may be something that we have not really experienced yet.

The fact is that whatever the masses are fed upon will be the result of what the masses produce. If we feed animals rubbish all the time then they will eventually lose strength, energy, die younger and have reduced brain power. We are doing exactly this to ourselves and I say we only have ourselves to blame because we begin the cycle ourselves by watching the programs, reading the magazines and listening to the radio stations. Once trapped into the cycle we will find it difficult to get out again, because we more than often do not even realize we are in it. Because this banal nonsense works on the masses we all have no choice but to switch off or join in. There are precious few outlets left for those who know themselves and think for themselves. We are already losing strength and energy and the masses certainly are experiencing reduced brain power, as governments reduce school targets and the media lower their standards daily to accommodate the power of the mass buy.

As if to prove the point of the effect upon the brain I recently did an experiment. I had flown back to the UK from a grueling trip to California, where I had spoken on hundreds of radio stations, TV shows and lectures. My mind was weary with all the effort and I was exhausted with repeating the same thing over and over. I needed a small break and so I took a trip into the countryside to recharge my batteries. We, as a family had a lovely time and whilst away I had space to contemplate. The routine of the past few days, the travelling, the rushing around, all faded away and I was again balanced out with nature (the force). My mind was perfectly energized and I sat for hours reading a good book. But then the thought struck me that I ought to now try a polarity experiment and so when I returned from the break, and having no promotional activities to do for over a week, I decided to rot in front of the television and watch the utter rubbish that makes up 90% of the viewing timetable. I purposefully did not read or spend my time communicating with the people that I normally did. I had reasons for this that I shall soon come to.

The effect of this week-long experiment was that my usually energetic mind slowed down to almost a full stop. I lost all will to get up and move. I fell in with the patterns of the sit-com, which at the start all seemed to be the same, following the same patterns and making the same jokes again and again. These patterns engulfed my mind and I allowed it to happen for the experiment. Thoughts of the esoteric world, of books, of secrets and history were a far-off land to me now. I was alone on an island supported by the morals and choices of thousands of actors, presenters and script writers. Whatever they said I mopped up like a sponge. They were, after-all, my only input for days. I am embarrassed to say that I even started to like a couple of the inane shows.

By the end of the week, the old me had almost disappeared and yet there was sufficient left to know that this was the end of the experiment and that I needed to jump back into the water and swim back to my reality. In fact, this was easier said than done. On the first day it was such a bind having to pick up a book and read and yet I knew I must, for I had a number of radio interviews planned and needed to regain my (sometimes) lucid mind. And so my drive and determination won out and I pushed myself to read and read. There was a book in every room and I almost desperately lunged myself into intellectual conversation with friends and family, who were all baffled by my strange nature. Eventually and almost right up to the first radio interview I came around and re-started my gray matter.

But what did this experiment reveal? And how does this work? Understanding the mechanics behind this perfectly natural issue will help us to understand our own mind and how we can stop ourselves becoming the lowest common denominator.

Neurons

The brain is a complicated thing and yet it is what makes us who we are. I can lose a leg or an arm and still be me. But I cannot lose my head and remain Philip Gardiner. But this experiment revealed that I can in fact lose my head without visiting the guillotine. I can lose myself in the world of others, in the world of the lowest common denominator and I can become a sheep, preyed upon by wolves. There must be a physical reason behind this loss of self and indeed there is.

When we read, we have to interpret the letters into words and the words into imagery or some other form we can comprehend - we have to turn the code into our own language. These words and letters are based upon symbols from ancient times and so they affect our deeper psyche also - pulling upon the archetypes within. These same archetypes made the symbols thousands of years ago when ancient man carved or painted them into rock. Now we see these symbols across time in the form of letters. S for instance was based upon the serpent or snake and in fact so too were a great many letters. These are archetypes our subconscious and even unconscious mind recognizes. This takes brain power to convert that which we see. When we use energy in the form of electromagnetism via our biological and chemical brain we open up pathways and reconnect older ones. We remember things we have learned and join the dots in our circuitry - keeping alive the mind and making it stronger and more efficient.

Everybody's brains are roughly the same size and yet we are not all of equal intelligence. The reason for this is because some open and keep open the neural pathways in their brain by usage. We also keep open our connection to the ancient archetypes within our minds. These are the things, symbols and images, ideas and concepts that we all share genetically via evolution. An archetype is an image from which a thing is made - it is the form inside of us that is manifested in the physical world as symbol, text, building, art or even music. It is the connection to the natural world and we therefore, by reading myths, fables and stories from times past, keep this connection open, because we unconsciously recognize this within ourselves. And so, by working our brain with the right things, such as reading, we remain alive and lucid. These connections are also aided by music, the right food and influences. These come with knowledge too, knowledge that we should read the right thing, listen to music that touches our archetypes and eat the correct food.

The other side of this peculiar coin are the moments when we stop working the brain. For instance by watching the television what actually happens? Well, we are fed everything we need to know (or not) and so we do not have to concentrate too much. There are no words to read and convert, as all of the conversion has been done for us. The words are spoken to us and we are entertained often with a musical background. The images we would use our brain - and thereby imagination - to create from the written word, are now images already created for us on the screen. We are using another person's mind to do our work. Whole armies of people have come together to create a series of images and sounds so that we don't have to. No longer do we read *Lord of the Rings* and imagine the little Hobbits and the beautiful Elves, instead we simply relax back let the world pass us by and let somebody else do all the work. This is not always a bad thing of course, but like most things in life, we humans overdo it. Even our modern news channels dumb down the news into short accessible bites that we can deal with more easily on a simple level. These short bites are sugar coated with images, graphs and pretty pictures to further assist our brain, so we don't have to think too deeply.

In today's world there are millions of battles fought daily between marketing men and advertisers, producers and directors, radio hosts and designers, all scrambling around finding the latest and most advanced method of producing an "experience" for the people - to grab their attention, keep their interest and form desires leading to actions. Alas the actions required are now more often than not to spend our money or move us to vote one way or another. They are manipulations of a brain that is not thinking for itself and therefore will do as it is told. This is why images, sound and feel are all created for us by the corporate giants - so that we don't have chance to think for ourselves and therefore follow like lemmings, however subtly this may be.

Of course there is nothing new or different here to what has been happening for an awfully long time. Every Sunday the masses would be crammed like sardines into Church where the priest would read to them. The masses were not allowed to read or learn Latin - this was the role of the elite. Instead the people had to believe what they were being told. More than that though, the bored or inattentive would find it easier to stare at the stained glass windows where depictions and images of the stories were relayed in simple form for the ordinary man to comprehend. Songs were created using repetition and alliteration ramming the message home and we repeated these "catchy" tunes in our minds, thus distracting us yet again from thinking for ourselves. Man did not have to think for himself and so followed blindly.

There is nothing different happening today. Instead of filing into Church on Sunday morning the people wake to the annoyance of the alarm clock which tells them what to do. They then pour a coffee full of caffeine - the daily fix. Over breakfast, instead of conversing and sharing with their family they sit like zombies and watch the television where they are fed yet more rubbish. They are fully prepared for the daily cycle of earn and spend, before they then try to wind down with alcohol and fall asleep watching yet more rubbish, whilst eating junk food.

Escape is so easy and yet so difficult. It is easy to say and yet harder to do. The first dilemma is how do we even become aware that we are in fact caught in a trap? There are a great many who know all about the trap, and yet are happy within it. This is no different to the film the *Matrix*, whereby Neo has to decide whether to take the pill that will free him from this dream world state once and for all. People are simply happy not to have to work the brain, especially when everything is done for them. Others, like Neo, see that the reality of freedom is much more liberating for the mind. Think about a rabbit. Let us assume that we have two rabbits in a cage. They seem perfectly happy. They eat the food we place before them and play with the toys. They happily watch the world go by. Now let us take one of these rabbits and set it free into the world of nature. Suddenly the rabbit realizes that it can run free and explore. It can interact with other rabbits and become excited at the new opportunities that this whole new world has placed before him. The rabbit that remains in the cage knows no different and so is not unhappy. Now let us go back into the wild and catch the freed rabbit. We place it back in its cage and what do we find? We find a rabbit who now gnaws at the wire, eager and desperate to escape once again. We may also find that this rabbit will influence the caged one and lead to revolution. Similar cycles have been found in the human world at large when freedom is tasted by the few and spread to the many, causing revolutions on a grand scale.

I am of the opinion that if the world of dumbing down becomes too oppressive for the human nature then we will have revolution upon our hands. My reason for stating this is simple.

Firstly that it has happened again and again in the past. Most, if not all, revolutions of mankind's history have been caused by one man or a few men finding freedom and then passing it on to others. They suddenly see, as if in a flash of light, that they have been oppressed by their leaders. Often in the light of our modern minds these historical oppressions seem obvious to us now, but at the time it was not so, because the people were living in the cage and not outside of it. Once the rabbit is out of the cage the freedom sighted spreads like wildfire and all the rabbits start gnawing.

The second reason for stating that we may one day have revolution is simple - nature. I am not talking about nature in the form of countryside, instead I am talking about force. It is the strongest force in the universe because it is the universe. It will, as a force, find balance. Let's look at an example in-order to understand what I mean.

In the beginning scientists tell us that there was a big bang (although disputed by some). There was an initial period of chaos and then ordered gases and solids began to emerge. Eventually out of this new order arose life. Nature, the force of the universe, found order and then life, it is the life-force. This same life-force or nature is within each and every living being, plant, animal, mineral, fluid - well in fact there is nowhere it cannot be. We are part of it. If that is the case then we follow it, because we have precious little choice. However bastardized we have made this force in the human conscious realm with our conscious dabbling, it is still the result of a natural drive. The drive to be alpha dominant for instance. But examples in nature show us that what is not good for the evolution of the species is eventually driven out or adapted. I am of the opinion that the dumbing down of the human species on such a wide and mass scale is not good for the evolution of the humans, which have, after all developed consciousness and free-thinking as a result of the forces of nature.

Today billions of humans exist on this planet of ours and it is growing by the day. We are storing up and creating a human bomb that will one day explode inwardly or outwardly as a result of the oppressive nature of our media and capitalist lead system. This is no different to why Russia exploded with the red revolution or why the French rose up against the oppressive Royalty. Islam uses this scenario as a tool to beat the West and would only replace it with another form of oppression in the form of the written word - the Koran.

It seems that no matter which period of modern history we wish to look at, the same forms of oppression and dumbing down have been utilized to great extent, whether by government, religion or Royalty.

But what can we do to escape this living Matrix? The first thing to know, is thy self. This self is trapped in the unconscious world, forced downwards by the conscious world of mankind. It's like this: close your eyes now and imagine you are walking down a country lane with your dog. You watch as he runs off barking at the birds. Now open your senses and hear the other noises, the sound of the wind in the trees, the distant cars, the autumn leaves crumbling beneath your feet. Do this whilst still concentrating on the dog. Now, whilst doing both of these processes, be conscious of everything within your vision. The trees, the branches, every single leaf; the bugs, the blue sky dotted with wispy white clouds, the gravel underfoot, the soil, the fallen trees. Can you possibly hold all this information in your conscious mind all at once? I can't.

Our brain has a function that closes down unnecessary perceptions. We may be subconsciously aware of these things, but only to send messages to the unconscious world and often for defense. For instance we may always be listening out for threats. But the unconscious world is aware of all this, works with it, is driven itself by the forces of nature. The conscious world cannot cope and closes down perceptions. This is why dumbing down human's works so well, because we all have so much to think about and do. There are just too many things for us all to concentrate on and so we entrap ourselves in the less sensory world, alleviating our minds of the pressure. But this is a false answer to the conundrum, because by allowing our minds to close off even more we in fact are able to deal with less and less, until eventually we are no better than caged rabbits. The conscious mind needs expansion by feeding it good food that teaches it to cope with the expansion and allows it to be one with the unconscious world - in tune with nature and the force of nature.

We need to break out of the cage and run around in the wild like a fluffy tailed bunny rabbit in world of freedom - for believe me, there are plenty of carrots for the picking.

Once we have understood this we can begin to find ourselves under the conscious realm. We need to sit calmly and open our perceptions to the person we are and not who we are told to be or try to be. I am not the many people I revere and adore, I am me and I am part of the natural force. I do not need another man to imagine my world for me or draw pictures in place of the written world. I have my own imagination and powerful thoughts that can discover the links to archetypes within my unconscious realm. Give me the real and full story, don't patronize me; give me something useful and fulfilling, not how to become a super-model or racing car driver. Let us be part of nature once again and stop fighting it with our silly ways. You never know, we may in fact find that we enjoy the freedom.

Chapter 8

Evolution

It is now time to turn to the driving force behind almost everything we have discussed. I know this will have creationists jumping up and down, and yet, whether we call it evolution or creation, the fact remains that there is a force behind all of nature that drives it forward - the need to survive and procreate.

From the plants which pollinate and produce seeds to the fish of the sea scattering their eggs far and wide, all life on earth, and probably on other planets too, feel drawn to reproduce. Humans are not exempt from this process and in fact today in the 21st century we have come to the stage where we have consciously developed some amazing techniques to help this process along, or indeed stop it in its tracks. It seems that almost every single invention man has created is employed in one way or another for the sexual drive. The internet, one of man's latest great leaps forward (or is it?), is full to brimming of sex websites, with all-manner of creative methods employed to entice and beguile. Understanding the nature of this force and its effects upon us will help us to understand ourselves and the constant cycles of our lives.

It is probably true to say that everybody reading this will know what sex is and what its original purpose was and so we need not visit that sticky situation. However, not everybody is aware of our sexual connections to the greater nature of the solar system and via it to the very universe.

Menstrual
Clues to the cycles of female menstruation can be found in the very etymology or meaning of the word. It means on the simplest level "the cycles of the month" and *month* itself comes from the

proto-Indo-European word *menes*, from the moon. So the very term, *month*, is derived from the word *moon*, which reveals that the very earliest months followed the cycles of the moon and not the sun. There were in fact 13 cycles or moons in the same way that there were originally 13 zodiacs (Ophiucus being the 13th). Patriarchal religions stamped the solar male dominated pattern upon society and so we have 12 months or cycles in the Western world, following the cycles of the zodiac related to the sun and not the moon. The 12 disciples of Christ, who was the solar force on earth, are a clear example of how this can easily be found in most major religions.

All of this is very clear and can be shown from the language and even archaeological finds, but what does it have to do with our own drives and desires? Well, it is said that the female cycle "coincides" with the lunar cycle - a statement that makes it appear almost accidental and divides us, or the female, from nature by mere words. The fact is that the tides of the ocean and even the subsurface movements of plasma are affected by the gravitational pull and cycles of the moon and we are beings of the earth. Humans are anywhere between 50 and 70 percent (and sometimes more) water and so we too must be affected by these lunar cycles. The whole cosmic dance is one in which we are all players and participants. As the moon moves around the earth in the opposite direction to our corresponding solar cycles, it affects almost everything on the earth. Females are especially affected by this motion. In fact the menstrual cycle itself follows the phases of the moon and it is believed that in times gone by when mankind was more in-touch with nature we were much more in-tune with our cycles. Look at it this way:-

Let us imagine a tribe made up of equal men and women, with a third being children. The females would skin the animals, make clothes, choose local foodstuffs such as berries and nuts and care for the young. The men would hunt for extended periods and produce the defense for the tribe against wildlife and other tribes.

Once a month the moon would enter a certain phase (waxing) and the females would begin the menstrual (moonstrual) cycle. Of course, hunting was often better done at night, because the animals would be more docile and as man himself was not a terribly big, ferocious and strong beast, he naturally chose night-time to hunt. Amazingly and beautifully this may have "coincided" with the menstrual cycles, which would make perfect natural sense, being a time when man was no use reproductively and was better out of the way. In fact in certain parts of the Middle East and Africa whole groups of women still menstruate virtually all at the same time and under a waxing moon. The men are kept away - it being a sacred time. The whole beauty and perfect balance of this relationship between man and woman, man and hunt, woman and moon, is a wonder to behold. The men would return on the full moon as the optimum time for catching prey. Ovulating with the full moon gives a woman the best chance of physical fertility as the full moon accentuates the time of Ovulation and so man returning with boosted testosterone levels via the hunt would obviously join with his partner at the perfect fertile time. Research carried out at St. Andrews University in the UK recently revealed that women in fact prefer more muscular looking men at their most fertile times in the cycle. The opposite of this being that in the infertile times they prefer more feminine featured males - men they can associate with. It is believed that this is all due to evolution - in that muscular men would produce healthier offspring, whereas more sensitive men would be better lifetime partners. But what does all this mean for us today?

The same cycles are still surging through our bodies. The moon still pulls upon our fluids, affecting our mood swings. The powerful force of the moon pushes and pulls whole oceans, affecting billions of animals on a daily basis and so the strength of this force must seriously affect our minds. But, our conscious world and human created cycles of hourly, daily, weekly and monthly life have come into stark contrast against nature itself. We are in fact battling with nature in so many ways, and here in the menstrual and sexual cycles of humanity we have found some incredibly imaginative methods of "self" control. We have in fact declared biological and chemical warfare on nature by introducing the paradoxical pill. Our arrogance tells us that we have won the battle and can stop the flow of the sea, like King Canute. And yet millions and millions of women suffer from all-manner of emotional instability crises because of the lack of natural balance - because we do not live at one with nature and understand it. The pill is supposed to use natural hormones to unnaturally affect our cycles - re-making them more regular. Cycles are very often irregular without the pill because we are out of balance with nature. We eat unnatural food, drink chemical drinks and rush around like headless chickens. A great many women feel they must battle with their male partners for alpha dominance because the feminine principle has been subjugated for so long. This causes women to often take on unnatural roles and cause stress.

Every cause has an effect and we have to live with it.

I have no issue with women doing anything they want. Instead I am simply pointing out what nature wants. We, as individuals must decide on what is best for us, for whatever we decide will have a profound effect upon those around us. The issue is, that to do battle with nature is to join the wrong army. There area great many ways of having sex and not having children without needing to pump our bodies full of chemicals. The problem is, our logical mind wants to reduce the risk factor all the time and for a great many people in the world the pill is the only answer, because of the lifestyles we lead. I am not preaching, I am simply pointing things out. These cycles affect us, we have battled against them and we expect to win.

But it isn't only females that have cycles. Men too follow the rhythms of the solar system. We call all these cycles, both male and female, biorhythms - the rhythms of our biology.

In the late 19th century a doctor by the name of Willhelm Fliess pioneered work on biorhythms and observed both 23 and 28 day cycles in many of his patients. He spent many years collecting data and believed that these rhythms were fundamental to man's life. He called these rhythms "master internal clocks" and stated that these clocks began counting from the moment we were born and only stopped at death. He noted that the 28 day lunar cycles was mirrored more in the female, whereas the 23 day cycles was a male cycles - although he did point out that mankind is basically both male and female and that both cycles affected us all. He noted how the 23 day cycle influenced vitality, strength and staying power - distinctly male elements he believed. The reverse of this was the 28 day cycle which governed sensitivity, intuition and love - elements we associate with the feminine gender.

More recent research has refined much of this, even down to hourly cycles. For instance the psychotherapist Jed Diamond authored a book called *Irritable Male Syndrome* which pointed out from over 10000 subjects that the stresses and strains upon man today are basically screwing up the male cycles and causing depression, aggression and anxiety. The male hormone testosterone for instance fluctuates 4 or 5 times per hour, causing mood swings. In the morning testosterone is higher than at night and there are even yearly cycles, such as higher testosterone in November than April, which may be a natural device to stop winter births. Of course, as Diamond points out, it is not the cycle which is the problem, it is the denial that there is even a cycle and thereby the man cannot be at fault for his mood swings.

The whole point of discovering the force of nature behind our lives is to openly accept that we are affected by nature and to find a balance with it. This can be with ourselves and our own cycles, but it can also be understanding the cycles of our loved ones too. If man and woman better understood the forces that were placed upon each other from within (hormones) and without (solar and lunar system) then we might have more understanding of each other. This is not to say that we can absolve ourselves of aggressive natures or depressive mood swings. No, we must understand who and what we are in relation to the world we create. This world of the natural drive is nature itself; the world we create around us is from within our imagination and is not natural. Who can say that being a high-flying corporate executive with a cell-phone glued permanently to our ear and a wireless laptop fixed constantly within our gaze is natural? Is it natural to spend half our natural lives in front of a television screen or searching the internet? We avoid relationships this way, because we cannot understand them. We absolve our responsibilities as animals on a wonderful world in perfect harmony with the sister planets.

Nature drives our emotions, from male tension to female depression, and we spend our hard earned money running off to see the shrink because we do not understand the most basic of natural concepts. If we did then we would eat the right food on a regular cycle instead of grabbing a burger in-between business meetings or dropping the kids off at the crèche. We would drink the right fluid and not pump our system with mind altering drugs like coffee and alcohol. We would maybe even learn how to set up a world-system whereby we all lived, breathed and worked for the greater harmony of our species - you never know!

Instead we use the cycle for darker ends. Cycles are monitored not just by doctors and New Age gurus. The leaders and business moguls of our world also spot an opportunity when they see one and use the rhythms of life to manipulate us all even more. We also use them to increase our yields, to fish the seas and unnaturally step nature out of balance by fooling around with chemicals in animals. Will we ever learn?

The arrogance of man - believing himself more powerful than

nature - is one that will be our own undoing. There was a recent documentary on television about a man climbing Everest. Nothing unusual there, but the title of the documentary did make me chuckle - Man V's Mountain. It was as if we were pitting ourselves against nature itself and believing that we could conquer the mountain. Rest assured, if nature wanted to get rid of that little bug on its skin called man, it most certainly would do. Let's turn to a tale I mentioned earlier in the chapter - the story of King Canute - and see if there is a lesson held within the text for us today.

Almost everybody in the UK, if not the Western world, will know of the tale of King Canute and how he tried to turn back the sea, but is everybody aware of the esoteric teaching behind this remarkable story? The tale is one we can easily learn today, especially as we attempt to turn back the tide of nature and control it.

The time is the 11th century and the Viking Canute (Knut) is King of Denmark, Norway and England. He was a very real King and his tomb can to this day be seen in Winchester, England.

But as with most monarchs and people in power there erupts around them all-manner of weird and wonderful folktales, many based upon the art form of propaganda but many also based upon the sacred teachings of esoteric societies. In this instance we have a little of both, as the tale erupted well after the death of the King and so was therefore Christian and monarchist propaganda and yet it was released by brothers who knew the esoteric truths.

The story goes that the courtiers of King Canute were so overwhelmed with his leadership qualities that they constantly adored him and praised his every move. One day Canute was walking by the sea with his courtiers praising him as usual. He eventually grew weary of this praise and decided he would teach them all a lesson and said:

"So you say I am the greatest man in the world?" To which they replied:

"O King, there has never been anyone as mighty as you."

"And you say all things obey my word?"

"Yes my lord, all things bow before you."

"In that case bring me my chair and we will go down to the water."

Although the courtiers were puzzled they did as they were told and the Kings chair was placed close by the sea.

"Very well Sea, I command you to come no further." Said the King.

Of course they all waited and as we all know the sea refused to listen to the commands of the King. Finally he said:

"Let it be known to all inhabitants of the world that the power of kings is empty, and no one is worthy of the name king except Him, whose will is obeyed by Heaven, earth and sea."

We do know that the real King Canute was a religious man, with many non-Christian Viking styled followers who had followed him to England and so he ruled a religiously divided nation. It seems he respected the Christian Church and spent a lot of time and energy rebuilding the various churches and monasteries, in this way showing his allegiance to the power of the Church and according to some [1] had early but distinctly Masonic tendencies – using the buildings as symbols of the Grand Architects power. In this fable however we may have a hint of Christian propaganda revealing that the King himself is subject to the power of God (and therefore the Pope) in the form of the waves. But, as this story is obviously a fable and in all likelihood not a true literal account, then we do have to find the reason for it and as with many things there are many answers.

The most often used explanation for this tale is that it proves that no man is above the law of nature, created by God, and this is very true, however there is depth here that is taught in several esoteric schools and never passed on to the uninitiated. I believe it is time for the true depth of this teaching to surface.

To understand exactly what we are talking about here we will have to alter our perceptions slightly. Firstly we need to understand that the King in the story could have been any King. It simply uses him as the figure-head, the role. The King is in the role of our consciousness and indeed he is the head of the State and our own head. This King is our male-dominated consciousness that is constantly boasted of. We build up our own self-worth with our own thoughts – here portrayed as courtiers - the courtiers of the mind. In our conscious state we believe that we are in charge, that we control our actions, that we can do anything. This is not necessarily a bad thing, but it can become so if it is out of balance with nature itself.

Inside all of us the power of nature surges like the sea and if we believe that we can control or turn back this powerful tide then we are indeed fools and not Kings. As an example I will create a fictional role. Let us say that my wife has a deep natural urge to nurture and care for young. She is attracted to puppies eyes and baby seals, as we all are to some extent. This is a natural urge and a good one. If this urge gets out of control or out of balance then we will end up with a house full of children and baby animals, but she curbs the desire and balances it out with her conscious knowledge. However, if she denies the power of the urge, the natural urge that sources through her very veins then she will be a mental and physical wreck because the natural urges will never cease and allow her a moment's emotional rest. She will be denying an essence that is from within the heart of the very universe – the essence of life and life-creation.

No man or woman on this planet can deny the natural urges that are within us, creating desires, loves, hunger and all-manner of emotions that when out of balance simply form an unnatural state and division and duality. When Arthur and Guinevere were split apart the land became infertile. When Solomon and Sheba were parted, Israel divided; and Robin Hood was nothing without Marion. We must be in union inside our minds with the natural world, with our natural state. We cannot fight it, but we must live with it in balance and harmony.

King Canute as our male conscious self was simply balancing out the worldly thoughts of power that we all have, with the knowledge of the power of nature to which we are all subject. In this way, when we too believe that we can fight our natural urges, then we need to think again and to understand nature for what it truly is. These urges are not those bastardized forms that excuse a man of rape, no, these are pure and wholesome. They can be easily recognized because they will be beautifully creative moments and will be in perfect balance with that wee-small-voice we know as intuition.

The outer shell we believe to be "ourselves" is in truth the creation of others, of time and our own experiences. The real you or I lies at the very center of our being and it is in perfect connection to the universe - for it came from the very heart of the universe in the beginning. The problem is that because of a lifetime of "input" we have lost the ability to see or hear it.

King Canute was indeed a wise King, a clever consciousness, as he knew he was only powerful because he understood nature and his place in it. His courtiers – the "input" – were fools, who did not.

Time and tide, wait for no man.

Notes

1 *Arcane Schools* by John Yarker

www.masonicworld.com/education/files/artjuno02/YARKERAS4.htm

Chapter 9

The Wheel

So we now understand that we are driven by the force of nature and that this force affects our moods and actions. It is used by those who would want power to manipulate us. Understanding our psyche at this very root level is a bonus to the marketing man who can recognize the drive and railroad us at an unconscious level into action. But just because we now recognize our own true nature and just because we know that we can be manipulated does not necessarily mean that we either want to escape the loop nor know how.

There may indeed be people reading this book who are still perfectly happy to follow the desires of a false society, eating hamburgers, watching porn and producing heaps of waste for future generations to clean up. To these people, there is little that can be said, until they come to a realization that there is more to the universe than themselves. Others will become and some probably already were, alive in their minds to a new concept of themselves – as powerful forces, creating order and chaos with the energy and dynamics of the big bang itself. Imagine that force within every atom of your mind and body. Imagine what good it can do if we visualize positive thoughts and of course the bad if we visualize negative thoughts. We are driven by a powerful force yes, but we all too often bastardize it and use it for wrong ends.

"In the beginning was the word, and the word was with God and the word was God."

This one perfect and thought provoking sentence from the Bible has been used for all-manner of arguments and yet now we realize the truth of who and what we are and indeed where we came from, does it have a more powerful meaning to us? If we consider that the "force" of nature is "God", then the "word" was the "thought" visualizing creation. The two were in perfect harmony. There could not have been a creation without the power and force of God and this force could not have found form without the word or thought. God without instruction from the word is a force with nothing to do.

All of this is relevant to us today, for the exact same process occurs in our own lives. We have the power within us to do such a lot and yet we often fail. We lack the will power to see a project through or help one another. We do not even realize that this force resides within us – that we have what our ancestors called God, inside our own mind. And so, without the realization of the God within, how can we even think about giving it instructions. The truth is that the God within us is our very self in connection with and in understanding of the force of nature. Being out of touch with this real side of ourselves and concentrating on the false side of ourselves, simply divides us from God.

So how do I connect to this inner divine? How do I recognize what is truth and what is still falsity?

There is no simple answer to this, because everybody is different. Even some of the greatest philosophers and free thinkers of the world have steered away from giving people a list of ways to find the true self and others have clouded it in such arcane language that one needs a degree in alchemy to comprehend what is being said. However, there are ways we can help to clear the clutter of our lives and therefore help us see what is around us more clearly and find a good mirror. There are many dangers in this process. The first one is simple and yet missed by almost everybody. When you begin the path away from the world built upon desires, greed, lust, envy and all-manner of other deadly sins, then you will leave behind friends and family who will watch you from their world in amazement, often fear and sometimes jealousy. Often they will say that you are becoming cult-like, as if you had joined the Moonies, but the fact is that the same effect can occur. You will become distanced from them in so many ways that you will in fact be astounded. Let's just take an imaginary trip down to the imaginary Mall with your imaginary friends.

We all agree to meet up at the Mall in downtown Santa Barbara. Nobody offers to give anybody a ride because we all have our own cars, four-by-fours and jeeps. In this first instance we are now highlighted to our natural connection because we suddenly feel "guilt" over the amount of wasted fuel and extra carbon emissions we are all producing for no reason. Being a friendly caring bunch of people we never really noticed before, but now we are "conscious" of the effect upon "our" greater family (i.e. nature) then the resultant outcome is guilt. We then move into questions of why we bought that damn big machine in the first place and realize that it was because we wanted to fit in with our peer group, look like Tom/Penelope Cruise/Cruz (and thereby wear an outer shell), be the alpha male/female and express our bastardized desires. Once we have recoiled from this shock of what we were before we became enlightened we then discover that we actually don't even own the hulking monstrosity and that we are tied into a decade of repayments that we will now never escape because the first eight years will be spent just paying off the interest, and by then we will have extended the period buying another car to "keep up with the Jones's".

All of this, and we haven't even entered the Mall yet.

So, let's assume we have squared up the sudden shock of what we have done, *for no good reason*, and have found the will-power inside of us to step out and drive to the Mall – assuming also that we have called a few of our friends and offered to give them a lift. There will probably be a million things running through your head as you now try to assimilate yourself to the world of the road, the signs, the advertising billboards, the crazy mad late and desperate people who cut you up while they run headlong around their own personal hamster trap. You somehow feel separate from all of this now, as if aloof. You will learn over time not to feel superior, for that feeling is pride and that always comes before "the fall." Instead you may feel pity and this will bring other emotions such as the feeling and desire to want to help others escape the rat race. This is energy that must be well-harnessed and not wasted. Wait, be patient, build knowledge and true understanding before you waste it appearing like a mad fool to the rest of society. You will help nobody by simply showing them that they are living a terrible lie and that it is neither self-fulfilling nor helpful to nature to carry on the way they are. The danger here is despair – that the individual will feel completely helpless because they are trapped. Well, they will have to get over it of course, because we all are to an extent – but simply pointing out a weakness and not also a strength is negative. In this book I have constantly striven to point out that we have a great and powerful force within us, waiting to be unleashed – we must all do this if we wish to open another's eyes.

Now, let's assume we have managed to arrive at the mall without crashing into that limo carrying the latest plastic surgeons experiment and without crying with laughter at the sign telling us that floors can be slippery when wet. We open our door and fall several feet from our all-terrain vehicle that only ever leaves the garage and drives to the Mall and back. Before us are a bewildering array of colorful signs enticing us in as if we were a long-nosed boy-doll escapee from a doll-makers somewhere in 19th century Bavarian Europe. If we see the world around us in this lighter way, then it makes living in it much easier.

Once we are lured within the sanctum sanctorum or the shopping arcadia we are met with an onslaught of color, smells and sounds. A mass of marketing man's dreams and bank managers nightmares. All around us our senses are being torn apart. Bright colorful and primal images entice the young; soft abstract shapes and smells draw in the old and thumping beats capture the teens. Which way to turn? Depends on who you are and at what stage in your life you are at. Either way, like cattle you are emotionally fed into the right stall ready for the slaughter. As somebody who now sees all this for what it is – a sensory overload of mind and wallet manipulation – you will have a wave of different emotions and thoughts surging through your nervous system. Females will cope with this much better than males in general, because this is more their home than the males – although in today's world these roles are merging by the second. The male will walk around constantly aware of dangers and threats – almost taking no interest in the goods. This goes back in evolution to when man would be the protector of the family group; he would have his ear to the ground and his nose in the air. He will be the one watching out for people walking into his woman or children; he will be the one conscious of distant noises and most likely he will have gathered where the exit points are long before they need to exit. The woman on the other hand is there for the berry picking – gathering fruits, foodstuffs and animal skins for the growing family and aware that good times don't always last and so building up the store. The children gather by the lake's edge, playing at being grown ups and building social skills; annoying the elderly who are there simply for the necessities of life to keep them going another year.

Of course, it is not so simple these days and these evolutionary drives are now fashioned into an ever finer role and I am over generalizing substantially in-order to make a point. The point is that if you are in a state of heightened awareness then you will see all these things and more for the first time. The walls will collapse and be replaced with trees and clear blue waters edge; the sky will look down upon you without the always present white streaks from passing 747's and all around you will be half naked men and women from ancient times thrusting spears into bison and weaving baskets. You will see people for what they really are. There will be no ADHD, no SAD and no anorexia, because people will just be people with the only issues in life coming from the natural world around them and not the unnatural world. They will hold dear the cycles of the sun and moon; they will move with the seasons and be at one with the breath of the earth; they will respect their elders for the skills and wisdom gained over the years and hold this knowledge sacred.

In a short few thousand years all of this would be lost and mankind would find itself in a world of utter madness, barbarity, starkness and filth. Modern man has little respect for the earth; for the seasons; for the elderly. Modern man doesn't even give a thought to his own future children and ruins and rapes the planet as if there will always be another one found in a Christmas cracker. And like the rolled up paper we find in every Christmas cracker this world of man is a bad joke of our own making.

But let's proceed. We have now overcome our initial emotions, whether outbursts of laughter or stomach churning convulsions of repulsion. We all decide to head to the central diner area for a coffee and muffin (or in my case a tea and teacake). Once there we snigger at the ridiculously imaginative array of methods used by man to get caffeine stimulant into the body and so decide on an orange juice instead. We all take a seat. Our new perspective means that we begin to observe what other people actually do. We notice that a couple of our friends are distracted watching a member of the opposite sex who is obviously flaunting his or her wares like a bare bottomed monkey. For some reason we find this amusing now.

Another friend is jabbering on about some sitcom they watched on the TV last evening as if it mattered what actors in an imagined world were saying and doing on that box of photonic lies in the corner of the room. You start to frown and tilt your head, wondering what is going on inside their mind. Then compassion sets in and you remember how not so long ago you too were enthused by something that you didn't even consider to not be real – let alone used as a tool to manipulate your thoughts. "Strange", you think to yourself, "how a perfectly natural form of social interaction has been taken over by an imaginary world created by Hollywood."

Eventually though, the lesson is learned – that an altered state of mind is now radically different to the one left behind. You were born into the world innocent – there was no original sin within you as the Catholics would have us believe. Instead we gather sins as we grow and hand over our lives first to our parents and then to our peers. We almost never think about taking back our own lives. We simply remain on the hamsters wheel running like crazed rodents without any thought about what would happen if we stopped. Well, now we have stopped and suddenly we are still and the whole world is spinning around us – you are God at the center of the spinning vortex. You watch your friends and family and want to help them take that step and put the brakes on, but you know you can't do it for them, because it is a state of enlightenment that must be achieved by ones self. They must be ready and have airbags fitted for the sudden halt.

You walk alone back to the giant machine you call a car and the rest of us call a tank. You drive it to the car sales lot and swap it for an eco-friendly simple machine that is your servant and not the other way around. The decision is made – today you will become the king of your domain; today you will take back charge of your own life; today you will accept the responsibility for your actions and thoughts; today, you will stop the wheel from turning and step off. This is the first step to finding yourself, being happier with yourself and being one with the universe itself.

Chapter 10

How?

Well, now we have a deeper understanding of our place, who we are, what is really going on around us, but what difference is it going to make to our lives? The answer is that it may just unbalance us and cause us to feel and be separated from the rest of society unless we can find balance and understand that we can cope with this new perception. This is not a new religion, nor really a philosophy, it is instead a new way of being. It is more than just thought, for it creates reactions physically upon us. We feel differently, our emotions may be fraught with the thoughts and we could easily start to worry and develop stress related physical ailments. As with everything in our lives there are two sides of the coin. On one side we realize a new freedom from the constraints of control upon our minds – we free ourselves mentally from the trap we have allowed ourselves to fall into. On the other side we may now have a free mind, but we are still humans in a human world and we may still have all those debts and credit card bills generated whilst under the influence of the worldly mind. We may still have friends from whom we now feel distanced and lack those kinds of friends that we might associate with. These are the classic symptoms any cult member feels, and it is little different now for us. Fear not, for we are not in a cult, in fact if we have understood the concepts in this book properly then we are far from cult members, for we shall join no State, religion or society that will wish to control us. We should remember that we have our own mind now and not simply replace one control with that of another. As the Greek philosophers told their pupils, do not accept what you are being told, test and test again for yourself.

The difference with members of cults and our new found

freedom however lies in the discovery of the self and not the replacement of one control with that of a cult leader. But how do we discover the true self and how do we remain balanced? Not easy questions to answer, but there are methods to enable us to proceed. We must be conscious at all times that the major part of this self discovery is our own sincerity with ourselves. If we are not honest with ourselves then we fail at the first hurdle. Don't care what anybody else thinks, they are probably deluded themselves and will only bring "opinions" that are outside of your self and not internal realities. So let's run through some of the processes that will help us.

Rubbish

We ought to by now have gathered that most of the mental and physical food we eat is utter rubbish. From the commercials on TV, radio, in magazines and newspapers to the internet; from commercially aligned television programs to dumbed down pap for the masses; from junk food and drink to drugs and immoderate abuse of alcohol – all these things are junk for our body and mind. If we fed nothing but rubbish to our pets we would shorten their lives, probably make them obese and slow-witted. We wouldn't do it would we? Not unless we were uncaring or stupid. And yet we do this to ourselves, our children and our friends all the time. We pull into the drive-through with the full knowledge that fattening, chemical laced junk food is completely wrong for us and the environment. A survival trigger inside our minds closes off these negative thoughts and hunger takes over. Now of course we ought to know better. We know that these companies are playing on the emotions and evolutionary desires within us. We know that their "messages" are contrived to soften the blow. We know that they clear huge rain forests to feed the billions of cows required for their burgers. We know that their food is having an affect upon our body and indeed our mind. We know that it will shorten our lives, make us obese and slow-witted.

So what do we do? We use that wonderful tool – the consciousness – to imagine a better way. We imagine the outcome of the shopping trip and that we shall probably be hungry by the end of it. We can therefore imagine that we ought to take a small healthy snack with us, or find a healthier and more sustainable option. If we all did this, then healthier and more environmentally conscious restaurants and food suppliers would all benefit and send a stark message to the fast food giants. We would actually be affecting a physical change because of our internal change! Imagine if everybody who read this book did the same for themselves, their friends and family. Imagine if say in the life of this book only 10000 people read it, each with 4 or 5 friends. Now multiply this for everyday that food is eaten and we have millions of meals affecting the world! That's a lot of burgers not being eaten; a lot of trees saved; a lot of good suppliers benefiting and it is a serious shot at real democracy at work – the mind of man speaks.

But why stop there? Why not also do this for everything we purchase? Why not do this for every internet site we buy from? Why not insist that corporations be more responsible. Our own sense of *sincerity* must drive this process and with our own *personal integrity* firmly in place we will be in the drivers seat for a change and not the corporations. Now we can begin to see how finding our true self and empowering ourselves can affect things for the good.

There are also the rules for living that we all believe we have to live by. We use these rules to work out our daily lives and explain the way things are. Not all these rules are good. For instance one rule that we all seem to have is that making mistakes is error. If we mess up we call it error and beat ourselves up for it. We cause ourselves distress and this knocks on to others as we then also beat others up who make mistakes. But is this true? Is it in error to make mistakes? In fact it is part of being human – it just is. There is nothing we can do about making mistakes, we will always do it, all of us. There is therefore no point in feeling inferior, stupid, worthless and distressed, because we made a mistake where another did not. That other person may appear perfect in our eyes, but they certainly do not in their own. Stop worrying about what other people think, stop worrying about making mistakes in life. Instead accept that we will occasionally mess up and learn from it. Also, stop blaming the mistake for your mood. We are responsible for our moods and emotions. If we decide to have a go at painting a portrait and it doesn't turn out as we envisaged, don't blame the paint or the easel; don't blame the sitter or the lighting and don't blame yourself. Learn from the outcome, but also learn that your attitude to the not-quite-perfect picture is more important than the picture. The emotions of mistakes can cause depression.

Let's look at it this way. If we believe we have failed, then we shall feel like a failure. If we believe we have given it our best shot then we are the best. The reactions can alter your very emotions and there is a process we can go through to affect our emotions and thereby our overall spirit. To change our attitude to life we cannot simply sit down one day and say "right now my attitude has changed." It doesn't work that way. Instead what we have to do is begin by thinking different thoughts and taking different actions. These alternative and more positive thoughts and actions to every issue (such as a mistake) will create different emotions within us, which will be more positive. These positive emotions will form a new attitude in life in general and soon our depressions, distress and angers will lift and it will be nobody's doing but our own. This is taking hold of our world and affecting it, just by thought alone.

But there is more wonder in this new thought process, for by affecting our thoughts, emotions and attitudes we will in fact emanate a new persona and this will affect others around us. Positive mental attitudes are proven to improve relationships and the spiral starts to run upwards instead of downwards. So remember, it is not the mistake that is the problem, it is our attitude to it. We are not necessarily responsible for everything that happens in our life, but we are responsible for how we react to it. We are responsible if we moan and groan all the time in front of our children and then cause a cyclic reaction within them. We are not responsible for the ridiculous amount of waste in the world, but we are responsible for our action and reaction to it, especially if there is an alternative and *we know* about it.

More Rubbish

But there is more rubbish than that which we feed ourselves. There is also the rubbish we give out all the time. There is the physical waste that we all produce. When we buy products we almost always have packaging too. What do we do with the packaging? Do we send it through the recycling process? Or do we just not have the time or inclination?

The same process is true of our world of the mind. We listen to all kinds of different comments and opinions. We watch the many and varied programs on the television and read all kinds of different viewpoints. It is what we do with these that our *personal integrity* must deal with. George Harrison once put it quite well when he called it the *Devil's Radio* – gossip. Whatever it is we take in, we have to decide whether it is of good value to the world and whether it is worth repeating. Ask the question – what good will this information be for anyone? Is it in the interest of the listener that we tell them about some malicious gossip we just heard? Question yourself too. Will this do your conscience any good? There is much danger in the repetition of rubbish. If we keep removing the packaging from the rubbish we buy and piling it up then we will end up with a world full of rubbish. And right now we certainly seem to have a world full of physical, verbal and mental rubbish.

You will, if you haven't already, notice this more and more.

For me this was one of the most interesting points of becoming more and more aware of the subtleties of language, communication and manipulation. I still sit in a café and listen to those around me with a smile on my face or a grimace. It is so interesting – almost like watching the monkeys at the zoo. I know, I know, there will be those in uproar at this statement because it is politically incorrect. But the fact remains, when one is or feels removed from society in this way, then one immediately becomes "politically" incorrect anyway and why should we care? Politics after all is the "science of government or control." If you are not mentally controlled by another, then you are not part of their politics anyway. In fact we can balance out this "attitude" with the thread that runs through all things – love. One of the strands of love is compassion and by having compassion for all the life in the universe – including humans – then we have a better attitude. We could easily become depressed and feel isolated by our conscious awareness of the cage we call society, but that would be our reaction and it would be an incorrect one.

If we have personal integrity in all things – from recycling to gossip – then we should not be trapped by these subtle and seemingly minor elements of our society. And this is often the problem for a lot of people – that they seem minor and of no harm. But we have all played "Chinese Whispers" when children. We all know that a small thing can be blown out of all proportion the more often it is repeated. Let me give you an example that happened recently within my own circle of friends. One of my friends is married and has two children. Following a dinner party he took his wife home and then dropped off another friend, who just happened to be female. A neighbor saw him dropping her off and giving her a quick kiss on the cheek. These are close friends and have been for many years. Had his wife been there, and not at home paying the baby sitter and getting the kids to bed, she too would have given the woman a kiss on the cheek. Nothing at all remotely sexual in the act. But this neighbor next day went down to the hairdressers where she told her friend about what she had seen. This second woman was the wife of our friend's husband – the one dropped off. Are you following this? Well, he was away on business, which is why he couldn't be at the dinner party. Next thing we all know is that he is flying back from his trip in a furious rage because his wife was having an affair with somebody and they had been seen having sex outside their house.

All of this because of a simple kiss? No, all of this because of gossip. The kiss is a loving and affectionate way of showing ones feelings and there is nothing wrong with it at all in this context. Friendship should be enjoyed and not worried over. By the time the husband had almost killed himself driving back from the airport he had resolved to divorce his wife and spend the rest of his life in misery. In the end, when he found out who the man was that had "had sex with his wife on the porch" he lost all his anger and spent half the night in fits of laughter. We still all have a good laugh of this today. But the point is that the Devil's Radio can be a much more serious issue and can cause, even at the most subtle level, all-manner of problems. Speaking rubbish leads to great big piles of rubbish, and nobody wants that.

Moaning

We all like a good moan every now and then – some more than others. There are obviously reasons for moaning and reasons why some are more prone to it. Upbringing and parental influence have a large part, as do particular hormonal influences. Things don't always go right and we often forget that we appreciate the good and exciting times because generally life can seem a little dull. Without the lows there are no highs. But becoming a more balanced individual helps to flatten out these seasonal trends. Firstly by recognizing those moments when we moan that remind us of our parents! This is not really the real self, it is the cloak of the parent. Once we recognize this and become aware of it, we will soon replace it with a wry smile and realize what we are doing. Secondly we have to wonder, like rubbish, what good the moaning is doing for anyone. Is it making you happier? Is it getting the problem fixed? If we are using moaning to get a point across and get attention for our problem, then why not consider finding a different and less cumbersome and negative solution? For instance we might think the issue through and see if firstly the problem is our own making; secondly whether the person we are moaning to can do anything about it anyway and thirdly, are we just ruining somebody else's day for no good reason. The best method, if we truly do need help, is to find a positive solution ourselves to the issue and ask your friends or family if they mind you throwing the solution past them. This is putting a positive spin on a negative issue, which may otherwise have been a tool for spreading yet more misery and woe.

Mood Swing

Part and parcel of moaning can often be the mood swing. Nobody is immune to this because nobody is a robot – at least not yet. Nature has a massive role in the mood swing as we have already observed. From the moon to the sun, from food to drink and from physical activity to life-changing events, the mood swing is a barometer of human emotion a method of seeing how all these things and more affect us. The problem is that most of us have no idea how to read these swings, either in each other or in ourselves. Men may wonder why they feel so aggressive in the morning and women be confused why they feel so very low. None of us sit there and think how perfectly natural the process is and that there may be very little we can do, other than be conscious of the effect, alter our thought and actions and thereby our emotions and attitude. By just being aware of the effect and by respecting the currents of nature's ebb and flow, we come into understanding and balance with it – i.e. our new thought has created an affect. Of course understanding each other's moods will also help out relationships. If the husband is more in-tune with the natural cycles of his wife then he will be more understanding and caring at the right moment. In the same respect if the wife understands the natural drives within man and helps him with them, then there may be less aggression on our roads.

Children too have mood swings and it is the responsibility of the adult to understand and care for the child. This caring does not mean accepting that a temper tantrum is acceptable – far from it. Instead we as adults are expected by the child to know better and to put them in their place. If we fail to show the child that such extremes need compassionate but firm handling then they will simply grow with these extremes into more and more extreme behavior. They want to feel loved and cared for. They don't want to feel like their behavior is tolerated by unloving parents. By showing them loving firmness at times of extremes, they actually feel that love and care and will eventually respond to it.

Meditate

OK, I know, you're all saying it, "not that soft New Age rubbish." But meditation is much more than the popular *mis*conception of the lotus position. In Old English meditation derived from *metan*, meaning "to measure"; in Welsh it is *meddwl*, meaning "mind, thinking"; in Proto-Indo-European it is based upon *med*, meaning "to measure, limit and consider." In short, meditation is simply the process of thinking about something or considering the measure or extent of an issue. In this way we all meditate on a daily and probably hourly basis. You and I have just meditated on the very word meditate.

To live in this life and to assimilate the huge amount of information our brain has to cope with we must meditate. There are minor meditations such as the one we have just done together and there are major ones. But the most important of all is the one when we find time and space for ourselves to think through how we are coping with the world and our own life in general. The trouble is that most people don't do this and more than we would like to believe are actually afraid of facing themselves and what they may find. If we are truly *honest, sincere* and have *personal integrity,* then we will not fear these moments of *self* discovery, but relish them. Once we have found the time and space to think and be with ourselves we may discover that we actually like what we find.

Of course it is not always easy for people to find some time alone. I know in a house with children that true time alone is a difficult equation to work out. My own space is in the bath. Often I will read, but these will be books that I find profound and in need of meditative understanding. Other, more surface level books can be read almost anywhere, but here I find the time to consider the words spoken and to judge them mentally against my own thoughts. It is meditation without the need for candles and lotus positions – which hurts my joints!

But that is my method. Others I know use Yoga, some use their bedrooms with a low light and a stick of incense to open the senses. Whatever bakes the bread I say! But don't stop cooking. Meditate often, especially during periods of moaning and mood swings – because you need to center yourself again and meditate on why you are moaning and understand why these affects are happening. You are also better sometimes being away from company that may not understand your moods.

The television is often something we use when we want to chill out. This desire to relax and watch television is actually causing a problem. The desire to chill out is natural and is part of our centering process, but we feed our brains consciously and subconsciously the mindless rubbish that appears on our screens instead of taking meditative (i.e. measured and contemplative) moments for our mind to find balance after a long day of hard conscious graft. Instead of making a cup of tea and sitting in front of the television to relax, we should take this time to contemplate and order the days events in a positive way. We can do this with the right books, with thoughtful music, good social gatherings or just with our own self in silence. Use whichever method works for you, but do not expect the sitcoms and soap operas on the television to order and balance your mind. This is a natural part of your daily cycle – the mind telling you to re-fill the batteries and by refilling them with rubbish from the television you are simply compounding and storing up problems within your mind. If we can find the time to watch mindless rubbish on television then we have no excuse when we say "I don't have time for meditation." We are in fact stealing time and balance from our own mind, which subconsciously knows it and we are therefore building up guilt and blaming ourselves.

Love

The one overriding factor in all things – love. It may sound like a kind of religious statement – God is love – but the fact is that when we find who we are we will recognize it's because of love. Nature is the driving force of evolution and this force is driven by love, the bonding element, the draw together, and so even the very atoms of the universe may be said to have love (are we not made up of atoms?) And so, if love is at the heart of evolution, nature and even the atom, then it will be the force inside of us too. Like anything else we conscious humans touch, it can become bastardized out of all recognition, but when we find true love we know it deep within us.

Recognize love and do not be afraid of it. In today's world love can and is something many people fear because they may have once shown it only to be snubbed. Have strength, be balanced, show love for the fellow living beings and for nature in general and nature will know. Hamish Miller, a dowser in the UK often shows people how the earth produces energy patterns, which can be quite simple and yet beautiful. Sometimes he asks the people present to send feelings of love to the earth where they stand.

These feelings are converted into wave and particle thought forms. When we think and feel the emotion of love, actual waves and particles of energy are released from our minds. Via quantum entanglement these particles, now being on the same wave length, entangle or "mate" with the particles of the earth itself, with nature, and the result is always mind blowing. When Hamish dowses the same area again, the patterns on the ground are changed and this time they are more complex and more beautiful, as if the subtle energy signature of the electromagnetic earth somehow respected and understood the message the people sent. How remarkable is that?

Whatever the scientific truth about all this, the fact remains that the energy of love felt by people for nature and for each other is much better than the general hatred we have around us today in a war torn world. We all need to do our bit and to spread the waves and particles of love everywhere we go.

Gnosis

Anybody who has read my books will know about Gnosis. It is one of the processes humans have developed over time to find the truth of love and God within themselves. The truth for us today and for better enabling us to move forward is the art of balance.

Balance is one of those words easily said and less easily done or understood. There are many times throughout the day when we ought to be balanced. In our judgements balance is essential. We must balance all the things we have learned with the issue at hand. Should I really give in and buy my son yet another game for his playstation or should I buy him something useful for his education? Should I sit for hours staring at web pages or should I spend time with my loved ones? Should I give in to my negative mood swings or should I see them for what they are, understand them and use love to overcome them? Should I have another drink? Should I watch more television?

All of these and many more are choices we have to make where balance can come into the equation. There will be thousands just like them and all will need objective and thoughtful balanced answers. But remember, we can only be truly balanced once we know the two extremes of the scale. On the one hand there will be one reaction and on the other the opposite. We should remain the upright in-between the two extremes, balancing them out, neither one, nor the other, but the one who controls the weights. The Egyptians had a scale used by the god Thoth to balance the weight of the Pharaohs heart against the feather of the goddess Maat – basically truth and justice. Can we say that what is in our heart is truly in balance with truth and justice? If it is, then what is in our heart will be love, for it is the only true balance.

Try to see our internal psychological world as if it were energy. The lights and electrical equipment in our houses all use the energy of electricity and this has to be controlled and well-balanced. If we overload the circuits by plugging in a machine that draws off huge amounts of power all at once then we will tip the balance of our household circuits and we will blow a fuse. The same applies to ourselves in both the physical world and the mental world. If we overdo it at the gym and fail to feed our bodies with the right kind of energy then we will blow a fuse too and something will fail. If we similarly try too hard to concentrate on one particular aspect of our internal world then we are in danger of neglecting the other parts of our mind. We need to have perfect balance in both the physical world and in the mental world. We need to meditate on the weak parts of our lives and make them strong and equal to the other parts, which may try to dominate. Let's look at an example.

Let us assume that I have bought an old farmhouse and stretched my finances to the limit by taking on a huge mortgage that we can just about afford every month. In the first instance we have added stress to our lives. Secondly we have stepped upon the hamsters wheel and now have to work harder and longer hours to afford the "home" that we probably will not have time to live in. But now we have bought the home that we fell in love with we realize that it is run down and needs fixing. We look at the roof and find that all the wooden beams need replacing. This alone will cost thousands and so we arrange for an overdraft, adding yet more stress. As we move through the house we discover that the electrics are out of date and dangerous, the floorboards are rotten and several windows need replacing. But we are trapped now and overburdened with debt because of a dream. In fact our dream is rapidly turning into a nightmare. We go to the bank and re-mortgage the property to the hilt and take on an extra part time job – locking ourselves into a massive repayment scheme for the next twenty-five years.

We are now in this situation because we have rushed and therefore not meditated and thought through the process and implications. We have not judged the balance of finances and we have not realized the implications of the mental stress this would all cause. Would we have been happier and healthier of mind and body if we had simply downsized a little and bought something we could easily afford? The answer can only lie in balance. Our weakness here was our desire for the farmhouse. We were not strong enough of mind to accept that it was out of our reach and this is the element we needed to meditate upon – to ask whether our true self needed this farmhouse in the first place and even why we were so engrossed in the idea of it.

At the end of the day if we eat the right food, ponder the right questions and strengthen the weak spots, both physically and spiritually, then we will be more balanced, but to do so requires knowledge and understanding and this is the end result of our search – true wisdom.

The result of this wisdom will be sincerity, personal integrity, humility, compassion and love. In all this we need the strength from within and only *will power* will see this come to fruition.

Chapter 11

Food for the Mind

Throughout time there have been a great many free thinkers and doers. These are people who recognized the truth of human existence and expressed their understanding in literature. The following pages are a collection of these thoughts that I have specially chosen to help us on our journey out of delusion and into freedom thinking. These are not words to follow, worship and create icons out of – that would defeat the object. Instead, these are words for meditation, words to ponder and think about in relationship to our own lives.

There is great truth in these words, but like all the other words ever spoken or written they come from within the mind of man and so they are never perfection – just some of the closest we have.

Read the words and if one sentence truly touches your thoughts then adapt it to your own thoughts and live with it for a while. You will discover that eventually you will even move beyond these mere words to a state of your own that holds more truth for yourself.

"Self-observation brings man to the realization of the necessity of self-change. And in observing himself a man notices that self-observation itself brings about certain changes in his inner processes. He begins to understand that self-observation is an instrument of self-change, a means of awakening."
George Gurdjieff

"With realization of one's own potential and self-confidence in one's ability, one can build a better world."
Dalai Lama

"If each of us sweeps in front of our own steps, the whole world will be clean."
    Johann Wolfgang von Goethe

"The first step in the acquisition of wisdom is silence, the second listening, the third memory, the fourth practice, the fifth teaching others."
    Solomon Ibn Gabriol

"One who understands much displays a greater simplicity of character than one who understands little."
    Alexander Chase

"The man of wisdom is never of two minds;
the man of benevolence never worries;
the man of courage is never afraid."
    Confucius

"The One manifests as the many, the formless putting on forms."
    Rig Veda

"Everyone thinks of changing the world, but no one thinks of changing himself."
    Count Leo Tolstoy, Russian novelist (1828-1910)

"To be nobody-but-yourself — in a world which is doing its best, night and day, to make you everybody else — means to fight the hardest battle which any human being can fight; and never stop fighting."
    E. E. Cummings, poet, artist, playwright and novelist (1894-1962)

"Know thyself."
    Inscription at the Oracle of Delphi in ancient Greece

"It is better to be hated for what you are than to be loved for what you are not."
    Andre Gide, French author (1869-1951)

"A man cannot be comfortable without his own approval."
    Mark Twain

"Who looks outside, dreams; who looks inside, awakes."
    Carl Jung

"Men can starve from a lack of self-realization as much as they can from a lack of bread."
    Richard Wright, American author (1908-1960)

"Enlightenment must come little by little-otherwise it would overwhelm."
    Idries Shah

"A man's true wealth is the good he does in the world. Beauty is eternity gazing at itself in a mirror. But you are eternity and you are the mirror."
    Kahlil Gibran

"Man is free at the moment he wishes to be."
    Voltaire

"If you dare to take up the banner of enlightenment, you will be attacked from all sides. From the inside you will be attacked by your own mind and from the outside you will be attacked by everyone else's mind. Anyone who dares to succeed automatically presents a huge threat. If true freedom is going to survive within you, you have to be willing to fight for it. You have to have a sword in each hand at all times. One sword is for your own mind and the other sword is for everyone else's mind. You must be ready to use them. Anyone who wants to be truly free must be willing to stand alone in the truth."

Andrew Cohen

"Believe those who are seeking the truth. Doubt those who find it."

Andre Gide

"Losing an illusion makes you wiser than finding a truth."

Ludwig Börne

"We are all but recent leaves on the same old tree of life and if this life has adapted itself to new functions and conditions, it uses the same old basic principles over and over again. There is no real difference between the grass and the man who mows it."

Albert Szent-Györgyi

"Before enlightenment - chop wood, carry water. After enlightenment - chop wood, carry water."

Zen Buddhist Proverb

"The fish trap exists because of the fish. Once you've gotten the fish you can forget the trap. The rabbit snare exists because of the rabbit. Once you've gotten the rabbit, you can forget the snare. Words exist because of meaning. Once you've gotten the meaning, you can forget the words. Where can I find a man who has forgotten words so I can talk with him?"

Chuang Tzu

"Think like a man of action, act like a man of thought."

Henri Louis Bergson

"You can't wake a person who is pretending to be asleep."

Navajo Proverb

"Alice came to a fork in the road. "Which road do I take?" she asked.
"Where do you want to go?" responded the Cheshire cat.
"I don't know," Alice answered.
"Then," said the cat, "it doesn't matter.""
  Lewis Carroll, *Alice in Wonderland*

"No matter where you go or what you do, you live your entire life within the confines of your head".
  Terry Josephson

"A thousand men can't undress a naked man."
  Greek Proverb

"If I make the lashes dark
And the eyes more bright
And the lips more scarlet,
Or ask if all be right
From mirror after mirror,
No vanity's displayed:
I'm looking for the face I had
Before the world was made."
  W.B. Yeats

"Who is more foolish, the child afraid of the dark or the man afraid of the light?"
  Maurice Freehill

"A thing, until it is everything, is noise, and once it is everything it is silence."
  Antonio Porchia, Voces, 1943, translated from Spanish by W.S. Merwin

"No snowflake ever falls in the wrong place."
   Zen

"The world always makes the assumption that the exposure of an error is identical with the discovery of truth - that the error and truth are simply opposite. They are nothing of the sort. What the world turns to, when it is cured on one error, is usually simply another error, and maybe one worse than the first one."
   H. L. Mencken

"Do not seek to follow in the footsteps of the wise. Seek what they sought."
   Matsuo Basho

"Illness is not cured by saying the word 'medicine,' but by taking medicine. Enlightenment is not achieved by repeating the word 'God' but by directly experiencing God. Talk as much philosophy as you like, worship as many gods as you please, observe as many ceremonies and sing devotional hymns, but liberation will never come, even after a hundred eons, without realizing Oneness, Wholeness."
   Shankara

"Enlightenment means life lived in accord with all the laws of nature."
   Maharishi Mahesh Yogi

". . . religious feeling takes the form of a rapturous amazement at the harmony of natural law, which reveals an intelligence of such superiority that, compared with it, all the systematic thinking and acting of human beings is an utterly insignificant reflection."
   Einstein

"Divine unity (tawhid) is the return of man to his origin, so that

he will become as he was before he came into being."
  Imam Abu'l-Qasim Al-Junayd 910 AD

"In the death of the self lies the life of the heart."
  Imam Ja'far Al-Sadiq - 8th century

"All know that the drop merges into the ocean, but few know that the ocean merges into the drop."
  Kabir

"If I have been of service, if I have glimpsed more of the nature and essence of ultimate good, if I am inspired to reach wider horizons of thought and action, if I am at peace with myself, it has been a successful day."
  Alex Noble

"Whatever is at the center of our life will be the source of our security, guidance, wisdom, and power."
  Stephen Covey

"He that never changes his opinions, never corrects his mistakes, and will never be wiser on the morrow than he is today."
  Tryon Edwards

"Day and night cannot dwell together."
  Duwamish

"Before eating, always take time to thank the food."
  Arapaho

"When we show our respect for other living things, they respond with respect for us."
  Arapaho

"Those that lie down with dogs, get up with fleas."
Blackfoot Tribe

"When you were born, you cried and the world rejoiced. Live your life so that when you die, the world cries and you rejoice."
Cherokee

"When the white man discovered this country Indians were running it. No taxes no debt, women did all the work. White man thought he could improve on a system like this."
Cherokee

"Our first teacher is our own heart."
Cheyenne

"All who have died are equal."
Commanche

"Man's law changes with his understanding of man. Only the laws of the spirit remain always the same."
Crow

"You already possess everything necessary to become great."
Crow

"Walk lightly in the spring; Mother Earth is pregnant."
Kiowa

"When a man moves away from nature his heart becomes hard."
Lakota

"Intuition does not always appear as the ingenious breakthrough or something grandiose. Intuitive thoughts, feelings, and solutions often manifest themselves as good old common sense.

Common sense is efficient."
  Doc Childre and Bruce Cryer, *From Chaos to Coherence*

"Never mistake knowledge for wisdom. One helps you make a living, the other helps you make a life."
  Sandra Carey

"Preconceived notions are the locks on the door to wisdom."
  Merry Browne

"Wisdom is knowing what to do next, skill is knowing how to do it, and virtue is doing it."
  David Starr Jordan

"Ours is a world of nuclear giants and ethical infants. If we continue to develop our technology without wisdom or prudence, our servant may prove to be our executioner."
  General Omar Bradley

"The most powerful weapon on earth is the human soul on fire."
  Ferdinand Foch

"There is only one-way in which one can endure man's inhumanity to man and that is to try, in one's own life, to exemplify man's humanity to man."
  Alan Paton

"When I discover who I am, I'll be free."
  Ralph Ellison

"When one door closes another door opens; but we so often look so long and so regretfully upon the closed door, that we do not see the ones which open for us."
  Alexander Graham Bell

"When you are inspired by some great purpose, some extraordinary project, all your thoughts break their bonds; your mind transcends limitations, your consciousness expands in every direction, and you find yourself in a new, great and wonderful world. Dormant forces, faculties and talents become alive, and you discover yourself to be a greater person by far than you ever dreamed yourself to be."

Patanjali (c. 1st to 3rd century BC)

"All that we are is the result of what we have thought."

Buddha

"Resolve to be thyself: and know, that he who finds himself, loses his misery."

Matthew Arnold

"Until you make peace with who you are, you'll never be content with what you have."

Doris Mortman

"The moment you have in your heart this extraordinary thing called love and feel the depth, the delight, the ecstasy of it, you will discover that for you the world is transformed."

Krishnamurti

"The shape of our lives is defined by our insertion into institutions and systems whose interlocking power generates the "virtual reality" we experience. Such 'knowledge' is so thoroughly a part of our worldview that it simply would not occur to most people to question it. Yet underneath this reality is another, subinstitutional reality in which very different responses are simply acted out. This is the reality in which everyone, until very recently, lived."

David Schwartz

"Believe nothing, no matter where you read it, or who said it, no matter if I have said it, unless it agrees with your own common sense."
Buddha

"Sometimes it feels like energy or electricity when it is moving in and through us, but spiritual power is really a distinctive kind of knowledge that is like the key that opens the door or the switch that starts the energy moving."
Frank Fools Crow - Legendary Shaman of the Teton Sioux

"The greatest revolution in our generation is that of human beings, who by changing the inner attitudes of their minds, can change the outer aspects of their lives."
Marilyn Ferguson

"Man would indeed be in a poor way if he had to be restrained by fear of punishment and hope of reward after death."
Albert Einstein

"Only in quiet waters do things mirror themselves undistorted. Only in a quiet mind is adequate perception of the world."
Hans Margolius

"The appearance of things change according to the emotions and thus we see magic and beauty in them, while the magic and beauty are really in ourselves."
Kahlil Gilbran

"Better keep yourself clean and bright; you are the window through which you must see the world."
George Bernard Shaw

"The eye sees only what the mind is prepared to comprehend."
Henri Bergson

"I cannot eat an elephant.
Yes you can.
How?
One bite at a time."

"If someone is too tired to give you a smile, leave one of your own, because no one needs a smile as much as those who have none to give."
  Rabbi Samson Raphael Hirsch

"I've never known any human being, high or humble, who ever regretted, when nearing life's end, having done kindly deeds. But I have known more than one millionaire who became haunted by the realization that they had led selfish lives."
  B. C. Forbes

"Kind words can be short and easy to speak, but their echoes are truly endless."
  Mother Theresa

"One man with courage makes a majority."
  Andrew Jackson

"In order to create there must be a dynamic force, and what force is more potent than love?"
  Igor Stravinsky

"We are, each of us angels with only one wing; and we can only fly by embracing one another."
  Luciano de Crescenzo

"You, yourself, as much as anybody in the entire universe, deserve your love and affection."
  Buddha

"The only real valuable thing is intuition."
Albert Einstein

"Trust your hunches. They're usually based on facts filed away just below the conscious level."
Dr. Joyce Brothers

"The be-all and end-all of life should not be to get rich, but to enrich the world."
B. C. Forbes

"What you leave behind is not what is engraved in stone monuments, but what is woven into the lives of others."
Pericles

"For a long time it had seemed to me that life was about to begin — real life. But there was always some obstacle in the way. Something to be got through first, some unfinished business, time still to be served, a debt to be paid. Then life would begin. At last it dawned on me that these obstacles were my life."
Fr. Alfred D'Souza

"Time is the coin of your life. It is the only coin you have, and only you can determine how it will be spent. Be careful lest you let other people spend it for you."
Carl Sandburg

"All animals except man know that the ultimate point of life is to enjoy it."
Samuel Butler

"Yesterday is a cancelled check; Tomorrow is a promissory note; Today is the only cash you have, so spend it wisely."
Kim Lyons

Chapter 12

Modern Man Myths

The books I have written and the documentaries I have made all relate to the history and mind of man. Nowhere have I embarked upon finding aliens, shape-shifting reptilian overlords or proving the existence of fairies, goblins, giants, ghosts or beings from other dimensions. And yet I am invited to speak at conferences and symposiums across the world held by UFO and Paranormal organizations; I am almost constantly talking on similar styled radio shows and write articles for magazines of the strange and bizarre. Why is this? Why does my work attract the attention of these elements of our society when I hardly ever comment upon them? To answer this, I have to delve into a world I have never before attempted to engage with – the world of the UFOlogist and paranormal.

It is with a mind of trepidation that I step forward into this world – for it is rife with division. In those moments that I have been involved in this, "arena of the strange", I have been amazed at just how much intolerance, bigotry and dare I say it, religion, there is in this field. I am not surprised, just amazed. The reason I am not surprised is because many of the supposedly unsolved issues arise from experience, and this draws man into a conflict with his consciousness. Experience gave rise to religion from the very earliest of times and it is no different today. We only have to look at Scientology, the Raelian movement and even the hard and fast beliefs of the adherents of David Icke, Eric von Daniken and Zacharia Sitchin to work that one out. In the past year as I write this I have been accused of being a member of the Illuminati, a Reptilian Shape-shifter and even a government stooge, sent to provide disinformation. When I stop laughing at these accusations I take a look at those doing the accusing and find most of the time that the individuals are steadfastly supporters of one of the above modern "religions." They dislike the fact that my work seems to always point back to the mind of man, and indeed it should, for this is the only place that mystery truly erupts. Nature has no mysteries – it does not care for them, if it cares at all. It is only mankind that brings the word "mystery" to things, for he himself cannot comprehend in his conscious state things outside of his learned norm. If the simple desire to get at the truth, from a neutral state, is being a member of a secret society that died centuries ago, or a disinformation agent for some dark and sinister government body, then I am guilty of the above. But the fact remains that I am none of the above. The truth, whatever that may mean, shall not be found in membership of some human created religion, whether it worships the illusion of a deity or alien. The truth can only be discovered when we come to a state of neutrality – when we don't care what the outcome of our search will be. If, on the other hand, we had an experience, then we are coming to the array of information with a pre-ordained mind. Take alien visitation for instance. I know a lot of people who have claimed that they have been visited by aliens or beings from other dimensions. Some of these individuals understand that the visit may not have been literal, but they are the few. The vast majority, like people who see ghosts, believe in the information that supposedly comes from their eyes. And why shouldn't they? Well, one reason is that a lot of the time these visions don't in fact come from the eyes at all, but from within the mind. We just assume they come from the eyes.

Experience then is a catalyst to religion and belief. We believe that what we have seen has external truth and therefore we move on and need to explain it and often this develops into religious structures and from there into intolerance. From the very first Shaman who sat in a cave and induced an altered state with some peculiar plant we have seen all-manner of weird and wonderful things. This Shaman believed in what he saw – he had no classical scientific reasoning of our modern educated times. But people still today believe in what they see – things, which do not differ from the visions of the Shaman except in name. Those people that I mentioned before who understand that what they have seen may not have physical truth are more often than not very knowledgeable people – they have insight into the mind. Part of the questioning I go through with people who have these experiences involves their depth of knowledge about the human mind. Those people who believe their experience to have physical truth more often than not have little or no knowledge about the workings of the psyche, let alone the historicity of the experiences. Their lives are physical and external, they lack understanding of who they are, and they rarely look inwards.

I know these statements will offend a great many people. I know that these beliefs are strong and willful, but we have to think the unthinkable if we are to get to the truth and there may yet be a fantastic and incredible explanation. How many of us can say that we have studied the human mind? How many have spent years delving into the history of these experiences? How many have grasped the truths of alchemy, gnosticism, philosophy and the world of the esoteric? Not many, and certainly a very small percentage of those who cling to physical realities for the tricks our evolutionary mind plays upon us. It is however true to say that once the experience has occurred, many people spend huge amounts of time, money and energy researching all of the above and more and so eventually come to terms with their experiences, one way or another. The bitter taste comes when someone plays upon this element of the human nature and creates new realities and explanations, often placing themselves as the new messiah of the cause. Some authors tell us that we need to be free – to escape the chains of a society created and manipulated by the illuminati or the shape-shifters and then place themselves before us as the sacrificial lamb who will lead us into freedom. They are in fact setting themselves up as the new religious leader, manipulating the minds of the buying public, giving them explanations that somehow make physical sense. Instead of telling people to think for themselves and to avoid falling headlong into a new faith like some love-jilted teenager, they trail a blaze of publicity and make fortunes out of blatant lies, whilst swelling the ranks or followers who eventually lose all sense of self.

I am in no way saying that society is not manipulated by groups of men who have a lineage stretching back generations within their secretive organizations. Nobody can deny the facts of history – that secret societies have often taken hold of power and formed new nations. The Freemasons, Jesuits, even the Illuminati have all been implicated in wrestling power from those who went before. But to say that these men are there because of their connection to other worldly beings or aliens and that they sacrifice children to Lucifer is stretching the imagination. All men are capable of all things, and people in positions of power will do almost anything to maintain that power and increase it. This may indeed involve creating or continuing age-old rituals and systems that appear strange to us today – but yet again, the truth points back to the manipulation of the mind and not the quantum ether.

The fact is that the relatively psychologically uneducated masses do actually believe in all-manner of phenomena and that this has been used and abused by those in power for millennia. It began with deities and today we are fed paranormal and other-worldly tricksters via the one-eyed monster – the TV. Before mass media, strange experiences were classed as religious or spiritual experiences. Today we are being led into alien and even quantum explanations. As if to answer how societies concepts of their internal experiences change we only have to look at the reporting of ghosts. In the early 19th century and before, people in the UK typically reported that they had seen the ghost of an ancestor or recently lost love one, but something changed and almost overnight armies of Romans, Vikings and celebrity dead were on the books. What changed? The education system. Suddenly the uneducated were being educated in the history of their land and culture and suddenly the experiences were adapted. New information had been fed into the mind of man and newly amended experiences flowed out. Today we watch the TV screens and see the exploits of Mulder and Scully or any number of other weird and wonderful "entertainment" programs. And today our experiences flow out as aliens and even quasi-quantum realities. The only thing that has changed in all these thousands of years is the explanation for the experience. The only thing that has remained, is the experience itself. And so our search needs to focus on the experience itself and not on the many faceted explanations that have erupted or developed over time. And yes, I know, there are people who are now choking on their coffees screaming at this book and thirsting for my blood, but I have to say, in no way do I discount any of the explanations that man has come up with throughout time – instead I am simply saying that due to the evidence we presently have the only truth that we can still rely upon is the experience and we must wipe the slate clean and come to the issue again in perfect neutrality. If, after all this, we find evidence for ghosts, goblins and aliens then so be it – I am neutral in my opinion.

So what is this experience? Well, as readers of my other books will know, this experience arises from the connection point between the conscious mind, which struggles hard to comprehend everything around it, and the unconscious mind, which just absorbs, reacts and controls our unconscious actions such as breathing. The unconscious mind is a mystery to us, because we are simply not conscious of it. We have to imagine what it is like inside this huge world below our gaze. And yet, within this underworld there lies a whole lifetime of experiences and inputs – a great many of which we are not even aware of nor remember consciously. All the information we have ever been subjected to and more besides is hidden away in this remarkable world. Occasionally people wander off into this world, in dreams and even lucid dreaming, whereby we become conscious of elements of our unconscious world. The Shaman, medicine men and often priests and mystics of our past would and did find ways into this world and they reported their findings as if it had some physical external or exoteric reality. Using drugs, dance, meditation, prayer, isolation and even pain, these "special" people would wander in and out of this Otherworld at will, claiming to do so on behalf of their people for healing, prophecy and all-manner of other reasons. This was the place of the deities, where archetypal knowledge was often passed to and fro. The truth is that within each and everyone of us there is a central core that is the same and from this core comes the archetypal knowledge – things that strike a chord, or resonate with our own central core. This core has been built over vast periods of time, absorbing information at the base DNA level in-order for the species to survive and improve. It is so raw in it's origin that it in my opinion has its base in the origin of the universe itself in a prime mathematical equation built into our very genes, which themselves structure our physical body and brain and thereby structures the way our mind's work. This is the reason we all share common experiences. However, it is not just the Shaman who can delve into the unconscious world – we too are constantly popping in and out with every second of our lives. Sometimes images that are perceived within the unconscious world are brought up into the conscious world, which then has to give some explanation for what has just been experienced.

This now explains a great many things. Firstly, this connection point between conscious and unconscious has a name, the hypnagogic or hypnapompic. It is in fact the point between awake and asleep - the gateway between the two worlds. Many of the experiences that are explained as ghostly visitations or alien abductions can be now seen to have emerged from this Otherworld of the mind. Do some research and you will discover that often these experiences happen in bed or near sleep, where a unique effect called sleep paralysis occurs (where our muscles do not work and so we "believe" we are tied or frozen to the spot). However, there will be ardent believers now shouting about the fact that not all visions occur near sleep, and many are wide-awake. Well, as I have just stated, the mind is constantly going in and out of this Otherworld of the unconscious, with every second or millisecond the wave of energy resonating in and out of consciousness and unconsciousness. We can be wide-awake and an experience "slip" into our consciousness – whether spontaneously or via suggestion, such as the preaching of a pastor or lecture of a paranormal expert or even the education system and television. Suggestion is subtle as we have seen throughout this book.

Of course, it may be that our unconscious world is as real as our conscious world, but this can be a circular argument and best left to a philosophical debate. Here we are looking specifically at real physical realities and the delusion of our mind upon ourselves and others. The truth is that if we come to this whole concept with perfect neutrality, if indeed we can, then we have to take this alternative argument into consideration. We have to accept that the experience has been around since man became conscious and so he either became aware of the intrusions of ghosts, goblins, aliens and otherworldly beings or these elements are creations formed because of the clash of consciousness and unconsciousness. There may of course be a middle way, a third state that explains much more...

One of the archetypal things that is seen in altered states of consciousness (i.e. delving into the unconscious mind) is the wave-form or as some people believe, DNA. This wave-form is the basis of all life, for without the wave there can be no energy – the two are one. This is archetypal, seen by all, because it is within all. Over the thousands of years of man's delving into the mind or Otherworld, he has used his imagination to form this into and from that external animal, the snake. It became the serpent of wisdom I have so often spoken about in my other works, because it brought with it wisdom from within – the voice of the deities residing within ourselves. This is a vision back in time so far that the mind staggers – it is a vision into the power that gave rise to the big bang itself – the pure energy of the cosmos that gives us life. Along the path towards this sacred vision come all-manner of other elements – all perfectly in-line with evolution and our own growth. For instance, the classical image of the alien is two large eyes set upon an oval face and mostly without color. When a child is born he or she is set by evolution to search for his mothers face. At this stage the baby is not geared to recognize color or hair and so looks for an odd shaped head with two large eyes. The odd shape of the head comes form the hair not being recognized. When we go into the world below our conscious gaze we see back in time and into our evolutionary instincts – our archetypal world - and so using modern concepts that have influenced us these shapes are given a new name – alien or gray. I know this does not explain all the sightings, but it does explain a great many and it is no stretch of the powerful imagination to seek out clues to the other images seen. For instance the tall "grays" or "elves" are the babies "long shot" – recognizing the human form amongst the myriad patterns and shapes around him or her.

So, even with this small example we can see that there are fascinating alternative reasons for some of the experiences we have. The sleep paralysis, serpent or reptilian forms, grays, emotions and even time dilation can find explanation in the root to our present day consciousness. The clash between the waking and non-waking world has for too long deluded us, and with the addition of those who would manipulate us by stretching our imaginations for their own ends, we are left with a feeling of emptiness. Because of this many will shrink back from rational explanations based in the science of the mind and cling to their own experiences as real.

We are drugged literally and drugged psychologically by the society we have. In my opinion it is time to go rehab and stand back from all that we are told. We need to reappraise the world we are told exists and do ourselves a favor – learn from nature and our place in it. Nature is a wonderful thing – a thing full of wonder – and we have lost all sense of connection to her. We have filled in the gaps of our knowledge with the power of the imagination and in doing so we have deluded ourselves yet again. But worse than this, we have opened up a gateway for others to further this delusion and revealed our own lack of knowledge. Whilst we stand in awe of the fabulous tales of reptilian shape-shifters and ancient astronauts we are gullible to the ramblings of those that would be our new messiahs. The same is true if we stand in awe of the scientist who would have us build with asbestos or the medical community who tell our mothers not to breast-feed. It does not matter from what quarter the lie comes, it is still a lie and yet how can we know that we are being fed a lie if we do not test the food? In all things we must be neutral – have no belief, but form opinions that can alter with evidence. As we learn our evidence grows or diminishes, but at least it will be somewhere on the road to truth. Whilst mothers continue to allow their youngsters to claim that they are in contact with aliens and are of special genetic stock, then they feed attention seeking natures and in today's society enlarge their own social circle and self-esteem; whilst we fill the coffers of the priest he will continue to preach insane notions of a dying and resurrecting god; when we seek the wisdom of those who appropriate it, we feed the ego's of cult leaders; while we believe those lights in the sky to be alien craft, then we do not look at our leaders extravagant spending on black-technology. Seek none of the above, remain balanced, test all things spoken and written by man, trust only nature and true intuition. These are the only lights in the sky we should seek.

Conclusion

Oneness

There is a lot of talk about the *Oneness* in New Age and alternative circles. The amazing success of the film *What the Bleep!?*, brought home to many the reality of the quantum world and the unusual state of perception that we exist in. But during the whole film there was no mention of our past. There was no indication whether ancient man had ever understood such so-called realities before the 20th and 21st centuries. Is this arrogance? That only we in the modern age can understand such concepts? Or is it a lack of understanding and knowledge of the mind of our ancestors? I decided it was time to discover whether ancient man could have possibly known about the quantum realm of *One*ness. But first we have to understand it ourselves before we can see the clues our ancestors left behind.

To our modern eyes the concept of the *One* or *One*ness is mystical and Eastern in origin and there will be found truth in this. But we can perceive this reality with our Western eyes. Try to imagine yourself as a grain of sand. You are nestled upon the beach, one of trillions and trillions of grains of sand. You are quite separate and yet also part of and similar to the whole. All you see around you are other grains of sand. But whilst you concentrate on those, you neglect to see the sky from which falls the rays of the sun that contain life and the drops of rain that feed the ocean that formed you. You do not see that those other grains of sand were formed in the same way as you and that they too come from the same rocks; you are all the same. And one day, in millions of years you will form as ancient sedimentary rock one again.

In this way, we are all formed by the same methods, with the same energy. We all eat the same produce of the earth and drink the same water. We shall all return to this same earth from where we came and the earth shall one day return to the universe from whence it came. Ultimately it shall all 'roll-up' in the Big Crash and all be one again. In truth, it is all one anyway. It is all inter-connected and via quantum entanglement every piece of information is everywhere from all time in one place and in every particle. Imagine that! It's like a hologram plate. When we look at it the picture placed there by light energy it is three dimensional. When we smash the picture into a thousand pieces, every piece has the picture of the whole! This is what the holographic universe is like, but this time we have more dimensions such as time itself. So imagine, you as an individual are really part of a multi-dimensional holographic universe where you are every-where in all-time!

Well, that's kind of what the *One* concept is about in a really simple way. We are all individual grains of sand, moving in our own space and time, but we are also related to everything else.

Our thoughts are wave forms, but in the quantum realm they are also particles. Every thought we have is formed by waves and particles. Particles cannot die, they exist forever. If they are destroyed then physicists tell us that the entire universe will collapse. And so our thoughts, as particles exist forever. But scientists also found that particles can entangle with other particles. Experiments have shown that the thoughts of humans can entangle with the thoughts of other humans, especially when they are emotionally close, such as relatives and friends – we are on the same wavelength. People who are therefore close to the oneness of nature may very well be entangled with the particles of nature – the force that drives us. Getting in touch with that natural part of our selves is therefore connection to the sub-atomic world of the universe. But more than this, as we discovered in Chapter 5, Professor James Gardner said recently that the universe may in fact be intelligent at the sub-atomic level – the quantum level and so we may be part of the mind itself. This is the realm of the quantum Oneness.

So did ancient man understand this principle and what lessons for us can we draw? For an answer to this I just knew from my own research that I should turn to my Sufi friends and their ancient wisdom.

There is a tale told by the 19th century Sufi master Ghuath Ali Shah and today re-told by Sufi masters across the world. To many the teachings mean nothing. They are just nice stories re-told again and again and have in the re-telling lost their value. But this is not true. Those with the eyes to see can understand the many meanings behind the tales and in this respect my years listening to and learning from various 'teachers' of the Gnostic loop, including Sufi's, has seen me in good stead. The tale I speak of is known as *The Four Travelers* and I will now myself in all humility to the ancient masters, re-tell the tale and offer some explanation for our modern eyes. Understand of course, that in each tale, there are many levels of understanding and so you can find truths within for yourself.

There was a forest, black as midnight and thicker than thieves. It was a favorite route for many, but suffered from highwaymen and robbers and so it was that four travelers found themselves needing to rest for the night, but fearful for their lives and possessions. They were good friends and three of them had been so for many years and so after discussion they decided to take turns to watch around the campfire. They settled down and the first watch went to a carpenter and wood sculptor. He sat for a while and then noticed a small length of wood and so decided to pass the time carving a beautiful image of a woman. By the time he had finished it was time for the next watch and so he placed the wooden lady down and woke his friend.

His friend was a tailor and after a while he too noticed the piece of wood and decided to make some clothes for the image of the woman. He produced a dress of silk and finished off with small leather sandals. Now it was time for him to sleep and he woke the next man who was a jeweler. Again to pass the time the jeweler decided to adorn the little figure with beautiful jewels. The final watch was summoned, but this time the man, a new friend the others had met on the journey, had no skills at all and so felt very ashamed of himself. He saw the wooden lady and admired the art and craft of his new friends. He wanted to show that he too was capable of improving upon the wood. He decided the only thing he could do was to seek the help of God and so he prayed:

"Oh, Almighty and Merciful Lord, give us some portion of your glory and as the Giver of Life bestow upon this humble figure the gift of life."

The fire finally went out and all was dark, all was one black place. Then the sun rose and crept across the landscape, revealing the countless forms that had been part of the darkness. One of these forms was now new to human life – the wooden woman was a living, breathing creature. The four men now awake were aghast and in awe at their creation. The wood carver admired the contours; the tailor was gushing with pride at the serene silken dress and the jeweler thought the fine gems were full of inspiration. And yet the fourth man claimed the upper hand for himself, because it was he who had asked God to provide the life force. In truth, the four men, who just the night before had been friends, were now sworn enemies, each one claiming ownership of this thing of beauty.

And so, because they could not decide who owned the stunningly mute female they made for the nearest town where they sought out the judge. Unfortunately the judge and the town's people simply thought they were fools and so sent them to see the king. Again, the king, thinking them to be fools sent them to the Sufi master who this time took all five out to see the Tree of Knowledge and with an assembled audience began to ask the tree for its wisdom. No sooner had the Sufi begun to speak than the tree opened up before them and as if by magic the young lady walked towards it and was swallowed whole. They never saw her again.

This marvelous tale reveals many 'truths', but I wish to concentrate on just two of them here. The fact is that the woman had come from wood and would therefore go back to wood. She returned to the place from whence she came, just as we all shall. This is the concept of the *One*. It is the unity of the cycle itself. Not only are we part of the whole whilst in this part of the cycle or that part of the cycle; we are the *One* before and after and always shall be. As cosmic dust, solar rays and universal energy feed our planet and us, so too shall we ourselves return to cosmic dust, solar rays and universal energy one day. We shall return to the place from whence we came, we are part of a great unified universe. There is no tomorrow, no yesterday, neither exist. The only place in time and space that exists is *now* and that is a slice through the whole.

But there is much more to this tale and for me there is a strong personal lesson for each and every one of us that can only be learned truly if we understand our 'place' in the greater whole. We are no different to that wooden woman. We came from the *One* into the *One* and so we are the *One*. Who is it that thinks they can form us, dress us and then give us life? Nobody owns us. To *own* is an anagram of *now* and in the now we exist. Whether your family, your town, your school, your employer or even your political or religious leaders – they all claim ownership at one time or another. And yet not one of them owns you just because they taught you, gave you life, gave you reason, clothed you or employed you. No ruler rules you. You are equal to everybody and everything else and no matter what another gives you it does not empower them above you.

You may be a small piece of the holographic universe, but within you is the whole picture right now.

This is the lesson that we all must learn from this book. That no matter what influences have preyed upon us and no matter how much we have wished to hand over the responsibility for our actions and thoughts, we are an equal part of the universe to everybody else and we share in our responsibility of it. No matter how much we believe in this god or that; no matter which political form we adhere to and no matter what experience we believe has formed our own personal belief systems, we are in fact at the root of it all an individual life form driven by the force and power of nature from which we came and to which we shall go.

Appendix

Terms

There are many terms used throughout this book and some not used but non-the-less still relevant and which may bring deeper insight into who and what we are. The following Terms are here as aids and guides to that deeper understanding.

Ablution

An alchemical term for washing a solid with a liquid. However the real meaning is to purge oneself of those things, which cause suffering, such as desire or ego.

Addiction

This is a condition whereby an individual becomes abnormally attached to something such as a drug, a concept or even a person. Often the individual requires the drug or concept in-order to function properly and requires psychological treatment in its absence. Intolerance, depression and extreme mood swings can often be the outcome of being separated from the addiction. The addiction may be caused by the person needing something 'extra' to fill in the perceived gaps in their life. The individual may appear decidedly **Bipolar**. Addictions begin for a great many reasons, but certainly they are connected to the lack of knowledge of self and balance in all things. Losing oneself to the materialism's of this world is a form of addiction to – being "hooked" on a TV program or needing the morning coffee are addictions and distract us from truth.

Agartha

This Tibetan word means 'the underground kingdom placed at the center of the earth, where the king of the world reigns.' It is evidently symbolic and is used extensively to imply the true center. This is a device utilized by the followers of the enlightenment experience for the central aspect needed to gain illumination.

AIDA

A term used by marketing specialists for ways of getting a message across and making a sale. A is for attention, I is for interest, D is for desire and the final A is for action.

Alchemy

Al or *El* is God or Shining. *Khem* or *Chem* is from the root Greek *kimia* and means to fuse. Therefore Alchemy means to fuse with God or the Shining – to be enlightened.

Basically it was a cover for the Eastern traditions, which ran diametrically against the Church of Rome and was therefore heretical. This is the reason for the obvious crossover of meaning hidden behind the subtle language of the alchemists. It was brought into Europe via the teachings of Geber (Jabir ibn Hayyan (721 - 815 A.D.)) among others. In later years the psychoanalyst Carl Jung concluded that alchemical images he was finding emanating from his subjects dreams and thoughts explained the archetypal roots of the modern mind and underscored the process of transformation.

Alkahest

This is the alchemy term for the power, which comes from above and allows or makes possible the alchemical transformation. Sometimes translated as "universal solvent" it is the concept of transmuting material (or mental) elements into their purest form. It is in essence the concept of revealing the hidden and true nature of mankind, which is the real "gold" of these arcane philosophers.

Anima and Animus

Terms developed by the psychologist Carl Jung and springing from the alchemists term for the soul. The anima is the feminine nature of the male and the animus is the male nature of the female. It was Jung's concept of the bisexual nature of us all and a reflection of the *"biological fact that it is the larger number of male (or female) genes which is the decisive factor in the determination of sex."* Memories, Dreams, Reflections, C. G. Jung (Vintage Books, 1989, page 391)

The anima and animus he believed manifested as archetypes in the dream or fantasy state, where the man's feelings were his feminine side and the woman's thoughts were her male side.

Archetype

Appearing as early at the middle 16th century the word archetype is derived from the Latin *archetypum* from the Greek *arkhetypon* meaning "first molded."

The psychological archetype (as opposed to the scientific) is the generic impulse or idealized object or concept. The words *stereotype* and *epitome* are often used as examples of the simplified archetype. It is the definition of a personality, for instance Father Christmas is an archetype seen in many cultures under different names and guises   all relating to one core arche typal concept.

Archetypes are used to analyze individuals, to ascertain their inner realities, that is, what is going on inside their unconscious state. The reason that this is so successful is because archetypes seem to be universal parts of the human unconscious mind – manifested in various ways, such as in the savior figures of Christ or Horus. These archetypes are within us all because they developed alongside our consciousness and conscious interpre-tations of the world around us – they are part of the whole human evolutionary life in the same way that an arm or a leg is.

Often these archetypes manifest in stories, fables, myths and today in popular fiction. Indeed most modern archetypal figures, such as Robin Hood or Superman can be found in parallel tales thousands of years ago. The most popular of these is of course the hero, a tale found related to the solar divinity and the resurrecting capabilities of the sun.

"... *it seems to me probable that the real nature of the archetype is not capable of being made conscious, that it is transcendent, on which account I call it psychoid."* The Structure and Dynamics of the Psyche (Collected Works of C. G. Jung, Volume 8), Princeton University Press, 1970, page 213.

Atman
This is the true inner reality, the Spirit or the "Son of God" element within each one of us. Alchemists say that the Atman does not die, is without end of days and is absolutely perfect.

Baqa'
Sufi term referring to the Divine Attribute of Everlastingness. It is opposite to **Fana'** or Passing Away. When the Sufi reaches the state of fana' he is leaving himself behind and then only the Divine Self remains.

Bipolar
This is often known as manic-depressive disorder and can cause mood swings and extremes of energy. The symptoms of the bipolar individual are more extreme and severe than the ordinary mood swings most people have and are often they result in broken relationships, loss of employment and poor performance all-round. The typical onset of a bipolar disorder begins around the teens or early adulthood – although this is not always the case. Unless properly diagnosed the individual is often unaware of their disorder.

There are many causes of bipolar disorder, however some scientists seeing a family link are looking for genetic causes, although this may in fact be down to a learning pattern within the family also.

As to treatment there are many drugs issued by health experts, however, understanding that one is bipolar in the first place is where we need to start. We can chart our mood swings on a daily, weekly and monthly sheet and use the evolutionary cycles we have discussed in this book to assimilate the cycles. Instead of taking drugs it may be that we just need to be honest with ourselves and those around us who can help us through the lows and highs. Often just talking can offload the stress of the disorder and tests have shown that psychosocial work such as this reduces episodes. In addition to this there are herbal remedies, such as St. John's wort, for which there is some evidence of its effectiveness, although these should only be used in consultation with a registered expert as it can cause a switch into mania in certain individuals. There may also be a thyroid issue (because this gland introduces hormones into the system) and this should be checked out with a physician. Getting into a good rhythm and daily cycle can often help.

Consciousness

"For indeed our consciousness does not create itself – it wells up from unknown depths. In childhood it awakens gradually, and all through life it wakes each morning out of the depths of sleep from an unconscious position. It is like a child that is born daily out of the primordial womb of the unconscious." Psychology and Religion: West and East, Collected Works of C. G. Jung, Volume 11), Princeton University Press, 1970, page 569.

Consciousness is the state we are in right now, because we are aware and perceptive. When we are no longer aware of things or thoughts then we are unconscious – although our unconscious state may very well be aware of what is happening around us. The conscious state is what we assume to be *us*, to be the real me and you, but this is only half of the coin (if half at all) and the rest of our real self is hidden within the unconscious world. When we think of who we are, we immediately assume it to be the person we envisage in our conscious state. Using archetypes and associations discovered in dreams psychologists tap into the hidden part of our mind. Some philosophers break consciousness down into experiential (phenomenal) consciousness and abstract (access) consciousness.

Consciousness is definitely part of the brain function, as we may lose limbs and still remain conscious, but the question *are we conscious after death* has always played upon the minds of the greatest thinkers, with little conclusion. Breaking the structure and actions of the brain down into hard science reveals that it is an organic structure enlivened by electro-magnetic energy of wave-particle transmissions across neural networks. That is, our conscious or unconscious thoughts are waves and particles created by energy escaping from atoms and entering the next. In fact this is the same as the very structure of our universe and so our thoughts are very much in-line with the greater universe – a concept said by Prof. James Gardner to be intelligent at the sub-atomic level. Waves may reduce and die, but particles may not and within those thought particles we have information stored during our entire lifetime, which may be entangling with particles in the greater universe in a "DNA feedback loop." In essence, there may yet be found in quantum physics what the philosophers have been searching for – life after death. (See *Gateway to the Otherworld* by Philip Gardiner, New Page Books, 2008)

Dharma
An Eastern word, Dharma is the innermost nature of every individual and is the true Being. It is the meaning of life. Man is not acting to his full ability if he does not know his dharma.

Dream
A dream is an experience of visions and sounds during sleep and

are doorways into our unconscious self. Within our dream state we often have experiences that would be unlikely in the conscious world and these will involve archetypes and represen-tations of who we are or who we believe we are. Lucid dreaming on the other hand is the conscious experience of the dream and can be most disturbing or indeed enlightening for the person experiencing it. Many spiritual seekers claim to have mastered lucid dreaming and thereby claim access to the Otherworld of the mind and indeed another realm entirely. In fact the two extremes, that dreams are reflections of our unconscious self or that they are mirrors to the world of the divine, are both aspects understood as Gnosis – the mystical experience of the divine in the self.

"One can, then, explain the God-image... as a reflection of the self, or, conversely, explain the self as an imago Dei in man." Psychology and Religion: West and East, Collected Works of C. G. Jung, Volume 11, Princeton University Press, 1970, page 468.

Dreams are powerful devices for the mind. They help us to come to terms with issues that have occurred during the day and may be a restructuring of the neural pathways that we are only partly sometimes conscious of – a kind of re-filing or defragmen-tation of the hard drive.

"The cause of dreams are seven. They are what you have seen, heard, experienced, wish to experience, forced to experience, imagined and by the inherent nature of the body." Charaka Samhita, 300BC.

"The dream is a little hidden door in the innermost and most secret recesses of the psyche, opening into that cosmic night which was psyche long before there was any ego-consciousness, and which will remain psyche no matter how far our ego-consciousness may extend." Civilization in Transition, Collected Works of C. G. Jung, Volume 10, Princeton University Press, 1970, page 304.

In fact some philosophers believe that the dream state is the access to mankind's past, as our genetic history may be "remem-bered" as our evolution progressed.

Ego

Psychologically the ego is the destructive part of ourselves, causing suffering through desires etc, which lead to us making decisions about our life, which are at odds with the Inner Reality of Divinity. We can only eradicate the ego (or ego's) by realizing their effects upon us and our errors because of the force of the ego. Once we realize we have the ego or ego's we can set about removing it/them. Buddhists teach that we need to be free from the suffering caused by this element of our lives and give us a clear and distinct Eightfold Path to Enlightenment (which is the release):

Creative comprehension
Good intentions
Good words
Total sacrifice
Good behavior
Absolute chastity
Continual fight against the Dark Magicians – the alter ego's
Absolute patience in all.

Follow this path and be free from the sufferings caused by the opposites such as bad words, deeds and giving in to impatience.

Fana'

Ego death or the Passing Away of the self, leaving behind the Divine Self in Sufi tradition. The final element of fana' is the fana' al-fana', which simply means "the passing away of the passing away." This is the stage when the Sufi is no longer even aware of having "passed away."

Haqiqah

Sufi word for 'inner reality' and coming from the root al-haqq, which means 'truth.' Therefore, the inner reality of ourselves is in fact truth and truth is our inner reality, which can only be gained by fana' or the passing away of the self (**Ego**).

Insan al-kamil

The perfect man, the pure and holy one, or the universal man. This term is used in Sufism for the one who is a fully realized human being.

Jnana

A Sanskrit term meaning simply "to know" and related to Gnosis. Specifically the term refers to the enlightenment of the consciousness, or wisdom from within. The equivalent Tibetan word *yeshe* means, "to know the prime knowledge that has always existed" and this reveals the real meaning of the term Gnosis and Jnana as that inherent human and inner wisdom we can find by eradicating the ego.

Mandala

A Sanskrit term for a magic circle (also "completion") depicting the center of all reality. This center is the root of us, the goal of our objectives in finding the true self. Mandala's can be drawn personally by the individual as a tool to gaining deeper insight into their own psyche. Used in the East (Tibet etc) and of Hindu origin for meditation and contemplation, they are seen on buildings and in artwork and many buildings actually form three-dimensional mandala's on the ground, uniting heaven and earth.

In their generic form they are used to meditate on the cosmos, both metaphysical and physical. The square represented the Earth (e.g. the horizon as seen from the human perspective), which is called *Caturhrsti* meaning four-cornered. The "Star of David" geometric shape was used in the same way as it was in other parts of the world – to represent the union within of the opposite energies, the heaven and earth and the conscious and unconscious self. It is at least 10,000 years old and represents the balance required to escape from the materialism's of this world. That is, by escaping the material world, we find our true self and achieve nirvana.

Monad

The Self from Latin *monas* meaning "unity; a unit, monad". Man and woman are the physical manifestations of the spiritual monad and the divine monad resides in each of us as the Father, Son and Holy Spirit (Sometimes the Mother and feminine aspect and others, such as Dante's *Divine Comedy*, as the husband of the Divine Mother) – the Divine Triad. The objective of the monad is said to be self-realization.

Monism

The belief that everything in the universe is made of the same thing and that metaphysically all things are one and unified.

Nirvana

This is a Sanskrit word meaning 'extinction.' It is not heaven in the Western sense of the word, but instead a state of being, free from *Kilesa* (contaminants of the mind). These contaminants are not just materialism's, but also the deadly sins such as lust, hate, anger etc. To be free from these constraints one is in a state of bliss or happiness and hence nirvana. But this freedom must be total and consistent, which is the realm of nirvana, for transitory freedom (e.g., going back to *Kilesa*) is not true nirvana.

Buddha said that nirvana was deathlessness and the highest state of being, derived from good and right living. The opposite of nirvana is *samsara*, which is ignorance or clinging to *Kilesa* (the contaminants) in accordance with **Dharma**.

To the early Christians known as Gnostics, nirvana was no different to true gnosis or knowledge – the realization of the divinity within and the freedom from the state of suffering. It is neither coming nor going, neither up, nor down, but perfect, peaceful neutrality from all contaminants.

"Where there is nothing; where naught is grasped, there is the Isle of No-Beyond. Nirvana do I call it – the utter extinction of aging and dying." Buddha

The traces of this concept can be found emerging from India into Semitic (and Islamic in the concept of **Baqa'**), Egyptian and later Christian thought in gnosticism and then into medieval Europe via the hidden language of the alchemists. Alchemy was not about turning lead into gold, but burning off the contaminants of the mind and emerging phoenix-like in a state of true enlightenment. Opposed by the controlling elite within the Catholic Church, alchemy was frowned upon and yet allowed to continue as those in authority knew full-well that the ordinary man would not understand the arcane language.

"The destruction of greed, hatred and delusion is Nirvana." Buddha.

Persona

Derived from the Latin for "mask", *persona* is a social or character one plays and not the real self. It is also known as the *alter-ego* (Latin for "the other I.") We present our persona to the world as if it were truly *us*, and yet our unconscious and subconscious self realizes that this is a lie and so we torture our inner self with illusion. We take on the persona of others, such as when we are greatly influenced by an individual who may be a father or mother figure or an archetypal hero that we associate with. It is simply our way of dealing with the world and is derived from evolution itself – the learning ability within each of us in-order to better survive. There are issues with this drive though, especially when we do not realize what we are doing and eventually end up with a million different persona's that we not only confuse the outside world, but also ourselves. People actually end up believing that the persona or character they are playing is truly themselves and lose all sight of who they really are.

Others may believe the persona we display for a while, but eventually we will show signs of the inner reality and our mask will be cracked.

Psychosis

Several times in this book I have mentioned psychosis and so I needed to include it here because it can be misinterpreted. It is in fact a simple generic term for a mental state in which thought, perception and reasoning is impaired. Episodes of psychosis can bring about altered states of consciousness, hallucinations, lucid dreaming and cause people to have delusional beliefs. In this way, most of the world is psychotic.

Paradoxically, although the individual suffering from psychosis has strange visions (and therefore half the Prophets of religion were psychotic) and has altered states of awareness, he or she fails and refuses utterly to see the strangeness of their own actions and perceptions. This is a complete lack of insight and so the claim that the "Kundalini is enlightenment" can be completely wrong because instead of achieving an enlightened state away from the contaminants of the mind, the individual instead is distancing him or herself away from reality. Most psychotics and a great many people who have had psychotic (or sporadic Kundalini experiences) end up distancing themselves from others in society and have impaired social behavior. It is in fact a severe mental illness and is associated with **Bipolar** disorder and schizophrenia. People who are psychotic will often have deep mood swings, persecutory syndrome and depression and the causes can be varied, from drug and alcohol abuse to brain damage and even the Kundalini (an electromagnetic, chemical and biological effect within the brain). Research has shown that people with tendencies towards psychosis have increased activation in their right hemisphere. This location is responsible for our emotions, beliefs and paranormal attachments to explanations other people find ludicrous. [1] The same activity in the right hemisphere has been found in people who have mystical experiences and report paranormal activity such as ghosts, UFO's and even abduction cases. It may be simply that people who have different viewpoints to the norm are not anything like psychotic, it is just that they think using their right and intuitive hemisphere as opposed to the logical and ordered left hemisphere (used for constructs of mathematics etc). Many diseases such as multiple sclerosis can also cause forms of psychosis.

Treatment for psychosis is often medication such as antipsychotic drugs, but similar methods to Bipolar disorder such as cognitive behavior therapy, animal-assisted therapy and family therapy are growing.

SAD – Seasonal Affective Disorder

This is a cyclical recurring mood disorder revealing itself in mood swings, depression, lethargy and the need for sleep. The cycles occur seasonally, such as when there is less sunlight and is related to melatonin levels as these are often released due to sunlight. Therapy for these often includes bright light screens and some people have actually been drawn to moving abroad to more sunnier climes. The effect could be caused by the fact that we now no longer follow migratory patterns and move with the sun each season and the fact that we spend large amounts of our life inside. There are definite genetic issues here though as not everybody gets the disorder.

Shari'ah

The opposite of **Haqiqah** in Sufi tradition. Where *haqiqah* is the inner reality of the self, shari'ah is the outer reality.

Shaykh

A Sufi master. A shaykh or shaikh is a holy one who has realized his own self and can therefore becomes a guide for others. The female shaykh is known as a shaykha.

Sirr or Secret
Islamic term for the individual's center of consciousness, which is the source of ones own being. Only at this source center does one come into contact with the Divine Inner Reality. A fleeting glimpse of the Sirr is known as an *al-hal*. A permanent self-realization is known as a *maqam*, such as a Sufi Master.

Superconsciousness
A concept that assumes we can be more than just conscious of ourselves, but also conscious of our greater connection to the universe via being aware – i.e. conscious – of our unconscious self. The enlightenment process – the blinding flash of insight – is often linked to superconsciousness because individuals claim to have intense feelings of oneness to all things and incredible knowledge at a single moment in time. Unless understood properly and approached in perfect, all-encompassing balance, this often sporadic element of the human mind can cause neurotic tendencies and psychosis – as the individual no longer feels part of society, feels god-like, has depressive mood-swings and focuses entirely on re-entering the insight again.

Unconscious
We have very little knowledge of the unconscious, because we are simply not conscious of it. Doorways into the world of the unconscious as pointed out by Carl Jung and others are dreams and lucid dreaming (being conscious of the dream).

"Besides these we must include all more or less intentional representations of painful thoughts and feelings. I call the sum of all these contents the 'personal unconscious.' But, over and above that, we also find in the unconscious qualities that are not individually acquired but are inherited, e.g., instincts as impulses to carry out actions from

necessity, without conscious motivation. In this 'deeper' stratum we also find... archetypes... The instincts and archetypes together form the 'collective unconscious.' I call it 'collective' because unlike the personal unconscious, it is not made up of individual and more or less unique contents but of those which are universal and of regular occurrence." The Structure and Dynamics of the Psyche, Collected Works of C. G. Jung, Princeton University press, 1970, page 133.

What is therefore held within the unconscious state are those things we as individuals have picked up all throughout our lives and those things inherent within the mind of man, garnered over millions of years of evolution and in connection with the greater universe. This element of the unconscious world is "omnipresent" and identical to others – we therefore recognize these inner "archetypes" when expressed outwardly by the artist, musician, writer or speaker. Artists and others express this "mystical" impression because somehow (whether drugs or a special mental connection into the world of the unconscious) they have tapped into the "source." This is often how shaman, medicine men, priests and prophets have sometimes appeared to "know" so much about our selves and our world.

Notes

1 (*Lateralized Hemishperic Dysfunction in the Major Psychotic Disorders: Historical Perspectives and Findings From a Study of Motor Asymetry in Older Patients*, Schizophrenia Research 30 (27 (2-3)): 191-8.

Bibliography

The following bibliography includes all the books that have built my knowledge and given me sufficient insight to be able to lay down the preceding pages. I would recommend most but always say, read in balance.

Abdalqadir as-Sufi, Shaykh, *The Return of the Khalifate*, Madinah Press, 1996

Ableson, J., *Jewish Mysticism*, G. Bell and Sons Ltd

Alford, Alan, *When the Gods Came Down*, New English Library, 2000.

Allegro, John *The Sacred Mushroom and the Cross*, Hodder and Stoughton, 1970.

Appollodorus, *The Library: Greek Mythography*, second century BC

Baigent, Michael, *Ancient Traces: Mysteries in Ancient and Early History*, Viking, 1998

Balfour, Mark, *The Sign of the Serpent: The Key to Creative Physics*, Prism Press, 1990

Barrett, David V., *Sects, Cults and Alternative Religions: A World Survey and Sourcebook*, Cassell, 1996

Barrow, John D., *Theories of Everything*, Virgin

Bayley, Harold, *The Lost Language of Symbolism*, Bracken Books, 1912

Beatty, Longfield, *The Garden of the Golden Flower: The Journey to Spiritual Fulfilment*, Rider, 1938

Blaire, Lawrence, *Rhythms of Vision*, Warner Books, 1975

Borchant, Bruno, *Mysticism*, Weisner

Bouquet, A. C., *Comparative Religion*, Pelican, 1942

Broadhurst, Paul, and Miller, Hamish, *The Dance of the Dragon*, Mythos

Bryant, Nigel, *The High Book of the Grail*, D. S. Brewer

Butler, E. M., *The Myth of the Magus*, Cambridge University Press

Callahan, Philip S., *Nature's Silent Music*, Acres, USA, 1992

Callahan, Philip S., *Paramagnetism: Rediscovering Nature's Secret Force of Growth*, Acres, USA, 1995

Callahan, Philip S., *Ancient Mysteries Modern Visions: The Magnetic Life of Agriculture*, Acres, USA. 2001

Campbell, Joseph, *Transformations of Myth Through Time*, Harper and Row, 1990

Cantor, N. F., *The Sacred Chain*, HarperCollins

Carpenter, Edward, *Pagan and Christian Creeds: Their Origin and Meaning*, Allen and Unwin Ltd

Carr-Gomm, Sarah, *Dictionary of Symbols in Art*, Duncan Baird Publishers

Castaneda, Carlos, *The Teaching of Don Juan*, Arkana

Cavendish, Richard, *Mythology*, Tiger

Chadwick, N., *The Druids*, University of Wales Press

Clarke, Hyde, and Wake, C. Staniland, *Serpent and Siva Worship*, R. A. Kessinger Publishing Ltd

Cooper, J. C., *An Illustrated Encyclopaedia of Traditional Symbols*, Thames and

Hudson, 1978

Davidson, John, *The Secret of the Creative Vacuum*, The C. W. Daniel Company Ltd, 1989

De Martino, Ernesto, *Primitive Magic*, Prism Unity

Dodd, C. H., *Historical Tradition of the Fourth Gospel*, Cambridge

Eliade, Mircea, *Shamanism: Archaic Techniques of Ecstasy*, Princeton University Press

Epstein, Perle, *Kabbalah: The Way of the Jewish Mystic*, Shambhala Classics, 2001Fontana, David, *The Secret Language of Symbols*, Piatkus Books

Fortune, Dion, *The Mystical Qabalah*, Weiser Books, 2000

Frazer, Sir James, *The Golden Bough: A Study in Magic and Religion*, Macmillan Press, 1922

Freke, Timothy, and Gandy, Peter, *Jesus and the Goddess*, Thorsons, 2001

Gardiner, Philip, *Gnosis: The Secret of Solomon's Temple Revealed*, New Page Books, 2006

Gardiner, Philip, *The Ark, The Shroud and Mary*, New Page Books, 2007

Gardiner, Philip, *The Shining Ones*, Radikal Books, England, 2003

Gardiner, Philip, with Osborn, Gary, *The Serpent Grail*, Watkins, 2005

Gardiner, Philip, *Proof: Does God Exist?* Reality Press, 2006

Gascoigne, Bamber, *The Christians*, Jonathan Cape

Gerber, Richard, *Vibrational Medicine*, Bear & Company, 2001

Gilbert, Adrian, *Magi*, Bloomsbury, 1996

Goldberg, Carl, *Speaking with the Devil*, Viking

Harrington, E., *The Meaning of English Place Names*, The Black Staff Press

Hedsel, Mark, *The Zelator*, Century

Heindel, Max, *Ancient and Modern Initiation*, (1865-1919) The Rosicrucian Fellowship International

Howard, Michael, *The Occult Conspiracy*, Rider & Co. Ltd, 1989

James, E. O., *The Ancient Gods*, Weidenfeld and Nicolson, 1962

Jennings, Hargrave, *Ophiolatreia*

Jones, Alison, *Dictionary of World Folklore*, Larousse, 1995

Josephus, *Antiquities*, Indypublish.com

Jung, C. G., *The Undiscovered Self*, Little, Brown and Company, 1958

Jung, C. G., Recorded and edited by Aniela Jaffe, *Memories, Dreams, Reflections*, Vintage Books Editions, USA, 1989

Kingsford, Anna, *Clothed With The Sun*, London, John M. Watkins, 1889.

Levi, Eliphas, *Transcendental Magic*, Rider & Co.

MacCana, Proinsias, *Celtic Mythology*, Hamlyn

Meij, Harold, *The Tau and the Triple Tau*, H. P. Tokyo Chapter 1. 2000

Michell, John, and Rhone, Christine, *Twelve-Tribes and the Science of Enchanting the Landscape*, Phanes PR

Milgrom, Jacob, *The JPS Torah Commentary: Numbers* The Jewish Publication Society, New York, 1990

Miller, Crichton, *The Golden Thread of Time*, Pendulum Publishing, 2000.

Myer, Isaac, *The Qabbalah*, Kessinger Publishing, 2003.

Oak, Purushottam, *World Vedic Heritage: A History of Histories*, P. N. Oak, 1984

Oliver, George, *Signs and Symbols*, Macoy Publishing

Oliver, Rev. George, *The History of Initiation*, R. A. Kessinger Publishing Co., 1841

Pagels, E., *The Gnostic Gospels*, Weidenfeld and Nicolson, 1980

Paterson Smyth, J., *How We Got our Bible*, Sampson Low

Pennick, N, *Sacred Geometry*, The Aquarian Press

Piggot, Stuart, *The Druids*, Thames and Hudson

Plichta, Peter, *God's Secret Formula*, Element Books

Radin, Dean, *The Conscious Universe*, HarperCollins, 1997

Rees, Martin, *Just Six Numbers: The Deep Forces that Shape the Universe*, Phoenix, 2000

Roberts, J. M., *Antiquity Unveiled*, Health Research, 1970

Rohl, David, *A Test of Time: The Bible – From Myth to History*, Arrow

Rolleston, T. W., *Myths and Legends of the Celtic Race*, Mystic P, 1986

Russell, Peter, *The Brain Book*, Routledge, 1980

Schaya, Leo, *The Universal Meaning of the Kabbalah*, University Books, 1987

Scholem, Gershom G., *On the Kabbalah and Its Symbolism*, Routledge & Kegan Paul, London, 1965

Schwartz, Gary, and Russek, Linda, *The Living Energy Universe*, Hampton Roads Publishing, 1999

Seife, Charles, *Zero: The Biography of a Dangerous Idea*, Souvenir Press, 2000

Seligmann, Kurt, *The History of Magic*, Quality Paperback Book Club, New York

Sharper Knowlson, T., *The Origins of Popular Superstitions and Customs*, Senate

Signs, Symbols and Ciphers, New Horizons

Simon, Bernard, *The Essence of Gnosticism*, Eagle Editions, 2004

Smith, M., *The Secret Gospel*, Victor Gollancz

Talbot, Michael, *The Holographic Universe*, HarperCollins, 1991

Thomson, Ahmad, *Dajjal the Anti-Christ*, Ta-Ha Publishers Ltd

Turville-Petre, Gabriel, *Myth and Religion of the North*, Weidenfeld & Nicolson, 1964

Uleyn, Arnold *Reliositeit en Fantasie*, Baarn, 1978.

Vadillo, Umar Ibrahim, *The Return of the Gold Dinar*, Madinah Press

Wake, C. Staniland, *The Origin of Serpent Worship*, R. A. Kessinger Publishing Ltd

Walker, B., *Gnosticism*, The Aquarian Press

Watson, Lyall, *Dark Nature: A Natural History of Evil*, Hodder & Stoughton, 1996

Weber, Renée, *Dialogues with Scientists and Sages: Search for Unity in Science and Mysticism*, Arkana, 1990

Williamson, A., *Living in the Sky*, Oklahoma Press, 1984

Wilson, Colin, *Frankenstein's Castle: The Double Brain – Door to Wisdom*, Ashgrove Press, 1980

Wilson, Colin, *Beyond the Occult*, Caxton Editions, 2002

Woods, George, Henry, *Herodotus: Book II*, Rivingtons, London, 1897

Zollschan, Dr G. K., Schumaker, Dr J. F., and Walsh, Dr G. F., *Exploring the Paranormal*, Prism Unity

Other Sources

Dictionary of Beliefs and Religions, Wordsworth

Dictionary of Phrase and Fable, Wordsworth

Dictionary of Science and Technology, Wordsworth Edition

Dictionary of the Bible, Collins

Dictionary of the Occult, Geddes and Grosset

Dictionary of World Folklore, Larousse

The Apocrypha, Talmud, Koran, Bible, Dead Sea Scrolls - Damascus Document, The Community Rule, War of the Sons of Light with the Sons of Darkness, Messianic Rule of the Congregation, The Temple Scroll, The Writings of Pliny the Younger, Flavius Josephus, Pythagoras, Plato, Hippolytus of Rome, Ephraim the Syrian, Carl Jung, Jeremiah Creedon (Guardian), Foundation for the Study of Cycles, The I Ching (Richard Wilhelm translation), *The New Scientist*, Nag Hammadi Gospel of Truth, Gospel of Mary, Gospel of the Egyptians, On Baptism

BOOKS

O is a symbol of the world, of oneness and unity. In different cultures it also means the "eye," symbolizing knowledge and insight. We aim to publish books that are accessible, constructive and that challenge accepted opinion, both that of academia and the "moral majority."

Our books are available in all good English language bookstores worldwide. If you don't see the book on the shelves ask the bookstore to order it for you, quoting the ISBN number and title. Alternatively you can order online (all major online retail sites carry our titles) or contact the distributor in the relevant country, listed on the copyright page.

See our website **www.o-books.net** for a full list of over 500 titles, growing by 100 a year.

And tune in to myspiritradio.com for our book review radio show, hosted by June-Elleni Laine, where you can listen to the authors discussing their books.